# The Proper Stitch

## A Guide for Counted Thread

*by*

### Darlene O'Steen

~ *The Needle's Prayse* ~

*Symbol of Excellence Publishers, Inc.*

**The Proper Stitch**
**A Guide for Counted Thread**

The Needle's Prayse

Author: Darlene Garner O'Steen
Graphic Designer: T. Christian O'Steen

Symbol of Excellence Publishers, Inc.

Publisher: Phyllis Hoffman
Executive Editor: Barbara Cockerham
Editor: Diane Kennedy-Jackson
Production Vice President: Wayne Hoffman
Production Director: Perry James
Creative Director: Mac Jamieson
Executive Art Director: Yukie McLean
Art Director: Scott Begley
Photographer: David L. Maxwell
Photography Stylist: Jarinda Wiechman

ISBN:   0-932437-03-6

*About the covers:* Portions of Our English Heritage Sampler are shown enlarged on the front and back covers. See photograph on page 131 for the location of these sections within the design.

# Dedication

This book is dedicated to my partner, who shares the writing of this book, who shares the business, who shares my life and my love—my husband, Thomas Christian O'Steen. Thank you, Chris, for your encouragement and for always being there for me.

I would like to thank my parents, Wallace and Betty Garner, for instilling in me a sense of heritage and a love of family; my sister, Tammy Jones, for double checking my work; and my son, Patrick, for being so patient with his parents while we worked on "the book."

I would also like to thank the people at Symbol of Excellence Publishers, especially Barbara Cockerham, for being so wonderful to work with; and Phyllis Hoffman, for the opportunity to realize my dream.

# Table of Contents

*Reproduction by permission of the Syndics of the Fitzwilliam Museum, Cambridge, England*

*Reproduction by permission of the Syndics of the Fitzwilliam Museum, Cambridge, England*

# Introduction

*S*amplermaking has a long and rich history, which has been documented to as early as the 1500s. Although samplers are known to have existed in earlier periods, very few have survived the ravages of time. The sampler stitched by Jane Bostock, and dated 1598, serves as a foundation, or starting point, for many of the twentieth-century books relating to needlework and samplers.

During the sixteenth and seventeenth centuries, samplermaking was at its height. During this period, elaborate, eye-pleasing and fanciful stitches were used to create samplers that remain to challenge and inspire the needle artists of today.

Learning how to properly execute different stitches adds a new realm to the stitcher's creativity. By working added stitches in a multitude of combinations, a stitcher can create her own masterpiece, with additional texture and depth, and give otherwise plain embroidery a rich sophistication.

My love of embroidery and love of history goes back to my teen years. The visual appearance of samplers drew me to them, but it is the stitches used to create the samplers that have influenced me for the past twenty years.

I have prepared this book, based on the stitches and techniques used to create samplers through the centuries, so that I can share my fascination with stitches created more than four hundred years ago.

Although I have included a sweeping variety of stitches that have been documented to the sixteenth- and seventeenth-century heyday of samplermaking, I feel certain that passing years will note the discovery of even more sampler stitches. The materials and graphics presented in the book represent my efforts to be as authentic as possible with the stitch techniques but, as with most things in life, for most stitches there is more than one way to accomplish the same effect. I find embroidery to be very logical, therefore I have presented the most logical way of executing the stitches.

This book is designed to be a working reference for stitchers. The stitches included are grouped by families, based on similarity of construction. Each stitch is explained, with text and graphics. Many stitches are illustrated with photographs of antique samplers housed at the Fitzwilliam Museum in Cambridge, England. I chose to show only the portion of the sampler where the illustrated stitch appears, rather than showing the entire piece. There are many excellent books filled with photographs of samplers and I encourage you to study those books, and to visit museums for a firsthand look at early samplers.

Two sampler designs are included so that you can practice the methods of stitch making described in this book.

May each stitch you take be one of joy.

—*Darlene O'Steen*

# Chapter One

# *Stitching Techniques*

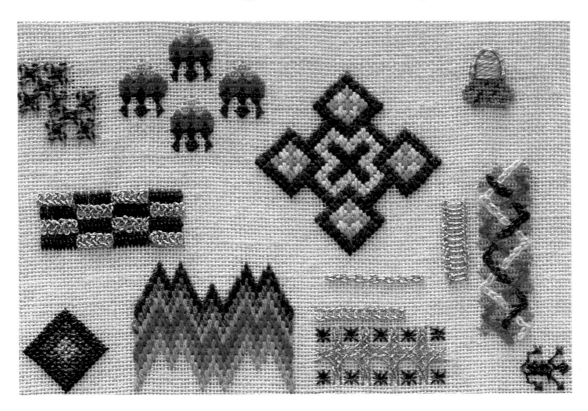

Since stitches are the basis of all embroidery, perfecting the techniques and skills required to work stitches will be beneficial to the needle-worker. This chapter contains basic information on using away waste knots, changing threads, and stitchery hints. The following chapters contain a wide assortment of counted-thread stitches that can be used to transform plain embroidery into a richly detailed and embellished work of art. Using the correct techniques, stitch numbering sequence, and positioning enables the stitcher to create designs using stitches that have a polished appearance. As you study and work each stitch, refer to this chapter for the instructions necessary to correctly begin each stitch and to change threads as the thread length is stitched into the design. It is often helpful to work stitches on a practice cloth before incorporating them into a stitchery project. Use your creativity and exchange fancy stitches that will occupy the same space in the design for plain stitches. Keeping a record of the stitches you practice, either in a notebook or on a practice cloth, will enable you to witness your progress as a needleartist. Let the information and stitch diagrams in this book open a world of endless stitch possibilities for you.

# Techniques of Stitching

Stitchers are often faced with uncertainty about the stitch techniques they use. Is the stitch being started and worked correctly? Does the sequence of the stitch progression really matter in the appearance of the stitch? What is the best method for changing threads?

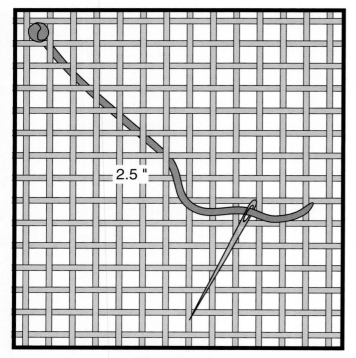

Illustration 1
Away Waste Knot, Version A

In this chapter, many of the basic techniques, including beginning and changing threads, are covered. These general instructions and methods are used over and over with various stitches. Many stitches are worked using the same basic techniques; however, certain stitches require specialized instructions, so each stitch is covered individually.

The working of any stitch can be divided into segments for ease of instructions. The following chapters include a variety of stitches, grouped as a stitch family for reasons that will be apparent. Each stitch is discussed, and methods are given for starting and working the stitch, changing threads as the length of thread has been stitched into the fabric, and ending the thread when the stitch row or section is complete. In addition, the appearance of the back is discussed, as an error in stitching can often be discovered quickly by observing the stitches on the fabric back. Turning corners, where applicable, is discussed. Special concerns for working a stitch are covered under a section titled "Difficulties and Hints."

## Beginning the Stitch

Most of the stitches discussed in this book are started by using an away waste knot. Although knots have become almost taboo in counted-thread needlework, the knots used to begin a stitch are later clipped off, and the loose thread is worked into the completed stitch. Using the methods described for away waste knots, versions A and B, allows the stitcher complete control over where and how the thread is ended.

## Away Waste Knots

Tie a knot at the end of the thread. With the fabric right-side up, insert the needle into the fabric a minimum of two- to two-and-one-half inches from the area to be stitched. If the stitch is to be worked from left to right,

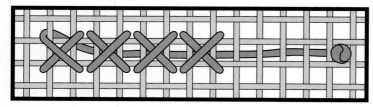

Illustration 2
Away Waste Knot, Version B

place the knot to the left of the stitching area. If the stitch is to be worked from right to left, place the knot to the right of the stitching area. To work an away waste knot, version A, carry the thread to the point where the first leg of the stitch begins. Leave a length of thread sufficient for rethreading the needle. Work the stitches required by the pattern, clip off the waste knot, rethread the needle, and secure the thread using the method described for the stitch. See Illustration 1.

Use an away waste knot, version A, to begin stitching in an area where no other stitches are in place, or where a new color begins. Use an away waste knot, version A, with pulled stitches to prevent thread from being pulled out of fabric during the working of the stitch.

An away waste knot, version B, is worked by placing the knot in the area and direction that stitches will be worked. Stitch over the anchoring thread, and clip off the away waste knot when it is reached. See Illustration 2.

## Changing Threads

It is important to change threads in a manner that does not detract from the beauty of the stitchery. Sometimes it is possible to see the location of a thread change because the flow of the thread has been interrupted. For example, when a thread is ended under the stitches just completed, tension on the thread creates a separation or pulled effect in that spot. See Illustration 3. This interrupts the flow of the stitch.

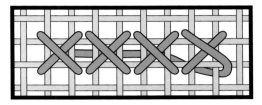

Illustration 3

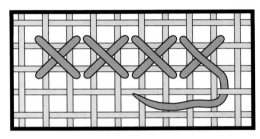

Illustration 4

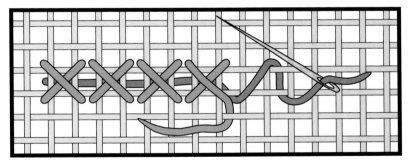

Illustration 5

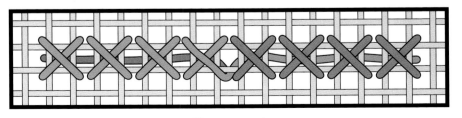

Illustration 6

To change threads, bring the old thread to the front of the fabric and "park" it in an out-of-the-way location. See Illustration 4. Thread the needle with the new thread. Run the new thread under the old stitches on the back of the fabric, and bring the thread to the front of the fabric in the appropriate spot to continue stitching. See Illustration 5. When the new thread has been used, plan to change threads in the manner described, and park the thread. Thread the needle with the old thread and run this thread under the new stitches on the back of the fabric. See Illustration 6.

**Hints**

1. Always try to end a thread color into the same color. Never end a dark thread color into a light color, because the dark color may be visible under the light thread color.
2. Never carry thread more than the space of one stitch (usually two threads) because the thread will be visible through the fabric when the stitchery is finished. For example, when stitching an alphabet, always end the thread after each letter is completed.
3. Neatness is very important to the finished appearance of needlework. End threads securely and clip close to the fabric. Long, loose threads sometimes work through to the fabric front and are found when framing has been completed. A neat back on a project gives a more professional appearance to the work.
4. Work with thread lengths no longer than 20–25 inches. Longer threads can look worn near the end of the length, from having been pulled through the fabric many times. This will detract from the finished appearance of the work. Shorter threads also tend to eliminate tangling.
5. Use the appropriate size needle for the work. The needle prepares the hole for the thread to pass through. If the needle is too small, the thread will become worn because the needle has not opened up a hole large enough for the thread, and the thread wears against the fabric as it is pulled through. If the needle is too large, the hole will not be filled by the thread, and will give a perforated appearance to the fabric.
6. Prepare the fabric edges before stitching to prevent raveling. Whipstitch the edge by hand; serge the edge by machine; or turn the fabric edge under ¼-inch and baste by hand or machine.
7. Add two to three inches to each side of the stitch measurement of the work to allow for framing, hemstitching, or the finish chosen for the piece.
8. To aid in correctly counting the placement of a band sampler, work a running stitch over and under two threads down the left side of the design area. This will aid in counting and will keep the work in line. Work one row across the width of the design and add a vertical running stitch on the right side of the fabric so that subsequent rows can be stitched without the necessity of counting.

# Chapter Two

# Cross Stitch Family

The stitches in this chapter are all based on the principle of crossed threads. Cross stitch, a true X-shaped stitch, with equal thread lengths crossing in the middle, is perhaps the oldest of all ornamental stitches. Found in ancient Egyptian and Hebrew embroideries as well as ecclesiastical embroideries of the Medieval Age, the simple cross stitch is viewed as the cornerstone stitch of modern needlework. Almost every culture has developed an embroidery form in which cross stitch forms the basic stitch. With the coming of the industrial revolution, cross stitch became the most widely used stitch for samplermaking. As many of the more intricate stitches of the 1500s, 1600s, and 1700s began to fall from favor, cross stitch emerged as the most-utilized stitch in the sampler works of the late 1800s. The versatile cross stitch was used on a variety of fabrics, and was used to form geometric patterns, alphabets, and borders on samplers of the past. Cross stitch can be equated with painting with thread. While many of the stitches in the cross-stitch family show crossed threads on the front of the fabric, several appear as crossed threads on the back of the fabric. The reversible four-sided stitch, used in the 1700s and 1800s to mark linens, shows a cross stitch on the fabric back. Herringbone stitch dates back to the Elizabethan and early Stuart eras, and is found in many fine needlework pieces of those times.

# Cross Stitch

The stitch illustrated has been called the English cross stitch, or sampler stitch. This is a general term for a specific type of cross stitch found in many English needlework books. To work this version of cross stitch, finish each stitch one at a time. Work all the cross stitches in the same direction. The basic shape of this stitch is an X.

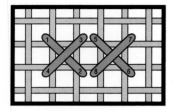

Illustration A

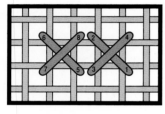

Illustration B

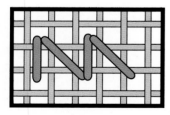

Illustration C

### Start
Use an away waste knot, version A, using the method described in Chapter 1.

### The Stitch
Begin this stitch by bringing the thread to the front of the fabric in the upper-left corner of the stitch. Continue by counting over two threads of the fabric to the right and down two threads, inserting the needle in the fabric at the lower-right corner of the stitch. Count up two threads and bring the needle up in the upper-right corner of the stitch. Count two threads to the left and two threads down, inserting the needle in the fabric at the lower-left corner of the stitch. To start the next cross stitch, bring the needle up in the upper-right corner of the cross stitch just completed and repeat the sequence. Illustration A shows this stitch worked from left to right. Illustration B details the stitch worked from right to left. Follow the numbering sequence to work this version.

### The Back
The back of this stitch appears as a sawtooth design. See Illustration C.

### Changing Threads
Use the method described in Chapter 1.

### Ending Threads
End the thread under the stitches on the back of the fabric.

### Turning Corners
Do not carry thread over long distances; instead run the thread under previously placed stitches to anchor, carrying the thread to the nearest appropriate corner to bring the thread to the front of the fabric.

### Difficulties and Hints
When working a design, do not turn the fabric for ease of stitching. All cross stitches must have the top diagonal thread laying in the same direction.

# Reversible Cross Stitch (version one)

Seventeenth-century samplers were worked using many reversible stitches; often it is difficult to distinguish the back from the front of a sampler from that period. Several methods of reversible cross stitch have been developed over the passing years. Version one of this stitch shows a cross stitch on the fabric front and a cross stitch with a slight variation on the fabric back. This version was often found in alphabet areas of samplers. Reversible cross stitches were also useful for marking linens and creating neat and attractive backs. See photo on page 118.

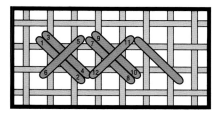

Illustration A

### Start
Use an away waste knot, version A, using the method described in Chapter 1.

### The Stitch
Begin reversible cross stitch in any of the four corners of the stitch. Repeat the first diagonal stitch so that two diagonals are lying side by side. The second diagonal places a diagonal stitch on the fabric back. The top diagonal stitch is placed with stitch 5 coming up in the corner that touches the corner of the next cross stitch to be worked. See Illustration A. Sometimes a double top stitch will be necessary so that a diagonal is placed on the back of the fabric. See Illustration C, stitches 37–38 and 45–46. To achieve a reversible cross stitch, in some instances the top diagonal of the cross stitch will not lie in the same direction on all stitches.

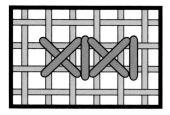

Illustration B

### The Back
The back of this reversible stitch appears as cross stitches with vertical (sometimes horizontal) stitches between the cross stitches. See Illustration B.

### Changing Threads
Use the method described in Chapter 1. Threads may be changed on the front or back of the fabric.

### Ending Threads
Run the thread under the stitches on the front or back of the fabric.

### Turning Corners
It is preferable that the top stitch come up in the corner that touches the next area to be stitched. Sometimes this will take planning ahead—for example, stitches 5–6 and 7–8 in Illustration A. This is not always possible to do. A vertical or horizontal thread will sometimes be necessary to reach the appropriate corner. See stitches 37–38 and 39–40 in Illustration C.

### Difficulties and Hints
Check the back of the fabric often when learning this stitch to make sure there are complete cross stitches on the back. It is helpful to visualize what is happening on the back of the fabric. Note that all cross stitches will not cross in the same direction. This allows reversibility and is not noticeable in a multi-stitch project.

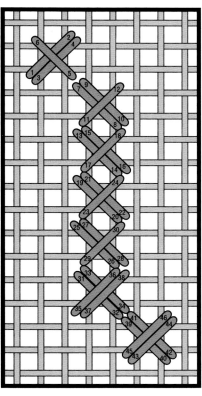

Illustration C

# Reversible Cross Stitch (version two)

To work this version of reversible cross stitch, finish each stitch one at a time. This unique method forms a cross stitch on the fabric front, and a four-sided stitch on the fabric back. It also serves the purpose of creating a finished look on the reverse side.

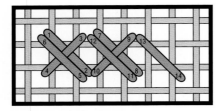

Illustration A

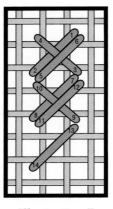

Illustration B

### Start
Use an away waste knot, version A, using the method described in Chapter 1.

### The Stitch
The stitch will begin in various corners. See Illustrations A and B. Not all diagonals will lie in the same direction on the top. This stitch works in a layered effect. For example, if the bottom diagonal goes from the upper-left corner to the lower-right corner, the middle diagonal will go from the upper-right corner to the lower-left corner. The next diagonal, or third layer, will go from the lower-right corner to the upper-left corner. Sometimes a fourth layer will be necessary to travel to a cross stitch that is turning a corner. This stitch will lie in the same direction as the second layer. See stitch 37–38 in Illustration F.

### The Back
The back of this reversible stitch appears as a square. The first stitch, however, will only have three sides. It is not necessary for all sides to be enclosed, although it is preferable. See Illustrations C and D.

### Changing Threads
Run the new thread under the stitches on the front of the fabric. Repeat the last stitch taken with the old thread and continue stitching as before. After the new stitches are in place, thread the needle with the old thread and run it under the new stitches on the front of the fabric.

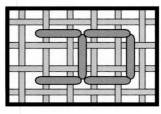

Illustration C

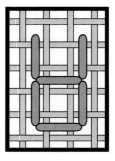

Illustration D

## Ending Threads

Run the thread under the stitches on the front of the fabric. If there is an open stitch in the area where the thread will be ended, carry the thread across this open area and carry it to the front of the fabric. See Illustration E.

## Turning Corners

When turning corners, the middle stitch (see stitch 3–4, Illustration F) should touch the corner of the next cross stitch to be worked. Sometimes a fourth layer is necessary to position the thread in the correct area for the next cross stitch. See stitches 37–38 and 39–40 in Illustration F.

## Difficulties and Hints

Check the back often to insure that the squares are formed properly. There should be no diagonals on the back of the fabric.

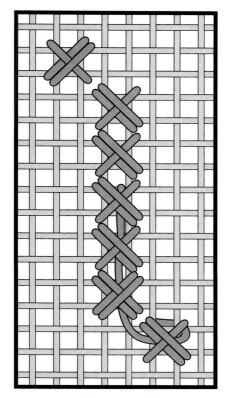

Illustration E

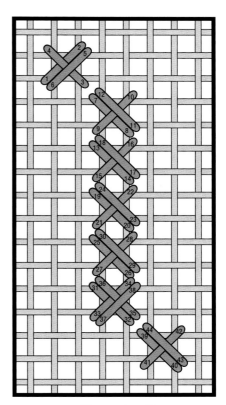

Illustration F

15

# Diagonal Cross Stitch

Diagonal cross stitch, because of its versatility, was a popular stitch during the seventeenth century. It is possible to create a smoother look on diagonals using this stitch rather than using cross stitch, and diagonal cross stitch has a much fuller appearance. This stitch works well with other stitches that are worked on the diagonal, such as queen stitch and Hungarian stitch.

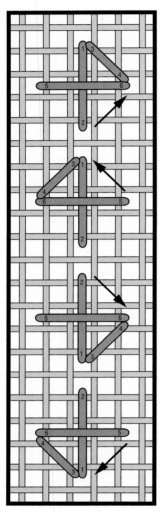

Illustration A

*Start*

Use an away waste knot, version A, using the method described in Chapter 1.

*The Stitch*

This stitch can be worked in four directions, each with variations. Diagonal stitch 3–4 changes position, depending on the direction traveled. A diagram is given for each direction. The main stitch is composed of three parts: Stitch 1–2 is a vertical stitch; stitch 3–4 is a short, diagonal stitch; stitch 5–6 is a horizontal stitch. See Illustration A.

Basic rules: If the line of stitches is traveling upward, start at the top of the stitch. If the direction is downward, start at the bottom of the stitch. The diagonal stitch is worked between the groups of vertical and horizontal stitches. Stitches 1 and 3 always share a common hole. To connect two diagonal stitches, count four threads up or down (depending on the direction the stitch is traveling) from stitch 6 in the grouping just completed and begin the same sequence of stitches. See Illustration B.

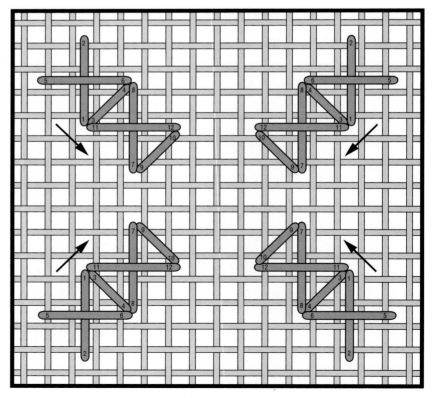

Illustration B

## The Back

The back of this reversible stitch appears the same as the front, except the short, diagonal stitch is missing. This gives the back a more open appearance. Note that the back of the stitch looks like a plus sign. See Illustration C for a view of the back of the stitch.

## Changing Threads

If the weave of the fabric is small enough, the thread may be ended under the stitches on the front of the fabric. See Illustrations D and E for ending the thread on the front of the fabric. Stitch G shows where the old thread is brought to the front of the fabric until the new stitches are in place. Run the new thread under the old stitches and enter the fabric in the designated area, carrying the thread to stitch 1–2 and continuing to stitch as before. After the new stitches are in place, run the old thread under these stitches. See Illustration E.

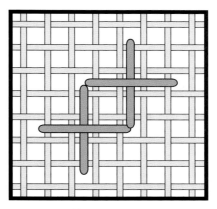

Illustration C

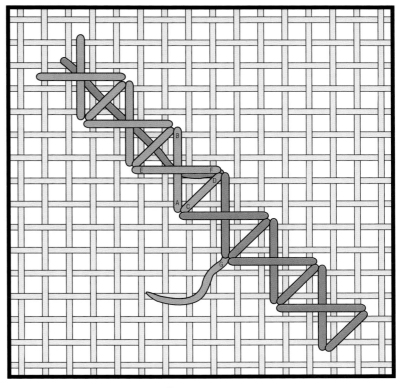

Illustration D

17

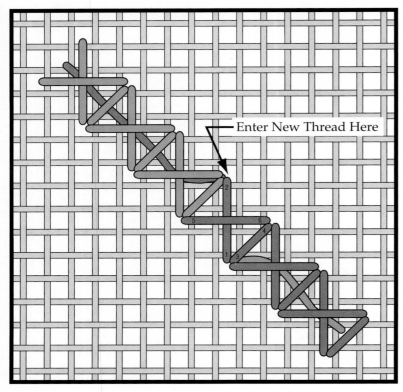

Illustration E

### Ending Threads

Run the thread under the stitches on the back of the fabric. When working this stitch with cross stitch, end the thread under the cross stitch rather than under the diagonal cross stitch. This will result in a more pleasing effect because the openness of the diagonal cross stitch reveals the thread more than the cross stitches. If the weave of the fabric is small enough, the thread may be ended on the front of the fabric.

### Turning Corners

Since diagonal cross stitch can only be worked on the diagonal, most corners will turn from cross stitch onto diagonal cross stitch. To move from cross stitch to diagonal cross stitch, complete all cross stitches up to the turning point. Count two threads from the corner of the last cross stitch in the direction of travel. For example, if traveling up and to the right, count two threads up from the upper-right corner of the last cross stitch. This will be stitch 9 of Illustration F. Continue to stitch the required number of diagonal cross stitches needed. When the last diagonal cross stitch is complete, notice that the short, diagonal stitch C–D can be used as part of the cross stitch. Make a

18

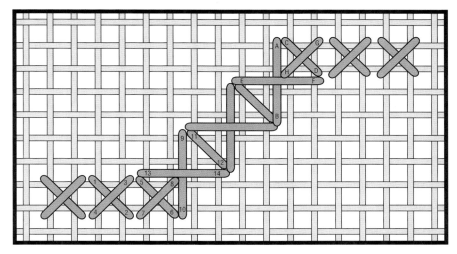

Illustration F

compensation stitch G–H to complete the cross stitch. The compensation stitch may or may not have the same direction as the other cross stitches. If desired, the compensation stitch may be slipped under stitch C–D to give the same appearance as the other cross stitches. However, this is not mandatory. See Illustration G for turning corners. This circle of cross stitch and diagonal cross stitch travels in a clockwise pattern. Illustration H demonstrates the use of a compensation stitch when a sharp turn is needed in a design. Stitch 7–8 makes the point complete by giving it the appearance of a cross stitch.

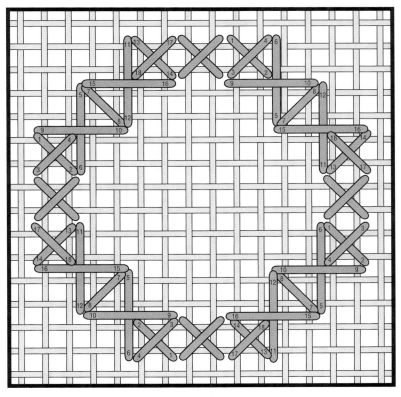

Illustration G

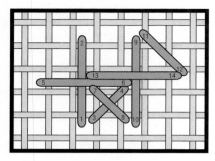

Illustration H

**Difficulties and Hints**
Determine the number of diagonal cross stitches required in a design by placing a cross between the symbols of the design that are on the diagonal. See Illustration I for placement of these crosses; each cross represents one diagonal cross stitch.

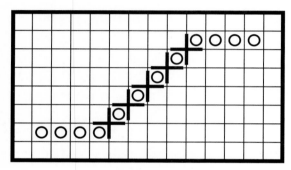

Illustration I

# Montenegrin Stitch (version one)

Montenegrin stitch, used primarily during the seventeenth and eighteenth centuries, reached its peak of popularity during the seventeenth century. The heavy appearance of the stitch was compatible with the ornate costumes that were popular during that time. Because the stitch is reversible, it was used to give a neat and desirable finish to stitchery.

*Start*
Use an away waste knot, version A, using the method described in Chapter 1.

*The Stitch*
This stitch is worked using three main stitches; a long diagonal to the right, a short diagonal to the left, and a short vertical stitch. See Illustration A. Illustration B shows the same stitch with two additional compensation stitches: A–B and C–D. Though not required, compensation stitches are used to give a finished appearance to the beginning of the stitch.

*The Back*
The back of this reversible stitch appears as a row of vertical stitches between cross stitches. The cross stitches do not appear as regular cross stitches due to a flattened appearance. See Illustration C.

*Changing Threads*
Use the method described in Chapter 1. Threads may be changed on the front or back of the fabric.

*Ending Threads*
Since the end of the row should have the same appearance as the beginning of the row, compensation stitches are needed. See Illustration D for compensation stitches E–F, G–H, and I–J. After the compensation stitches are in place, run the thread under the stitches on the back of the fabric. For a vertical stitch on the back of the fabric at the end of the row, bring the thread to the front of the fabric at I after completing stitch I–J. Run the thread under the stitches on the front of the fabric.

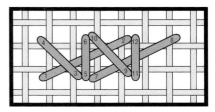

Illustration A

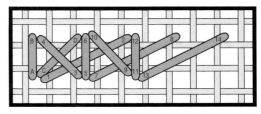

Illustration B

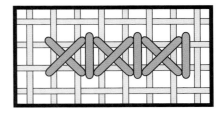

Illustration C

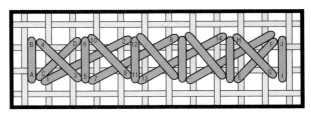

Illustration D

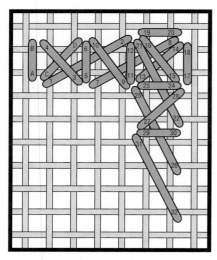

Illustration F

## Turning Corners

See Illustration E for turning an outside corner of a Montenegrin stitch; Illustration F details turning an inside corner.

## Difficulties and Hints

Montenegrin stitch has a very full appearance. It takes a basic pattern of three stitches to work this stitch. To recall all the stitches in the sequence, remember the following: long diagonal to the right, short diagonal to the left, vertical straight up. See Illustration G. To visualize this stitch in another way, think of the stitch as a fan opening from the left to the right, with all stitches coming out of a common hole. Begin with a short diagonal stitch to the left, and continue with a vertical stitch in the center, and a long, diagonal stitch to the right. See Illustration H.

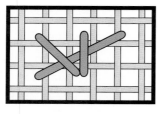

Illustration G

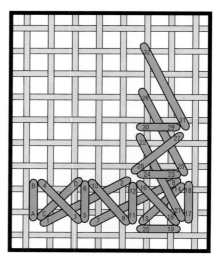

Illustration E

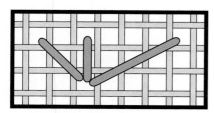

Illustration H

22

# Montenegrin Stitch (version two)

Montenegrin stitch, version two, has the same basic look as version one. This version, however, is worked using a technique more authentic to the seventeenth century.

### Start
Use an away waste knot, version A or B, using the method described in Chapter 1.

### The Stitch
This version is composed of the three basic stitches used in version one. The sequence of stitches is slightly different, giving the stitch a different, layered appearance. See Illustration A.

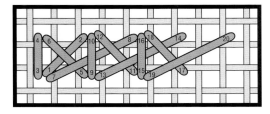

Illustration A

### The Back
The back of this reversible stitch appears as a row of vertical stitches between cross stitches. See Illustration B.

### Changing Threads
Use the method described in Chapter 1. Threads may be changed on the front or back of the fabric.

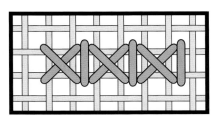

Illustration B

### Ending Threads
Run the thread under the stitches on the front or back of the fabric. See Illustration C for compensation stitches used to end the row.

### Turning Corners
See Illustration D for details on turning an outside corner, and Illustration E for turning an inside corner.

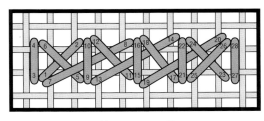

Illustration C

### Difficulties and Hints
Check the back of the fabric to verify that no stitch in the sequence has been forgotten. Due to the denseness of the stitches, it is difficult to see mistakes on the front of the fabric. If a stitching mistake has been made, the problem can readily be seen on the back.

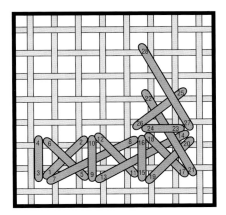

Illustration E

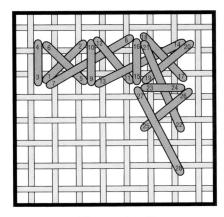

Illustration D

# Diagonal Montenegrin Stitch

Diagonal Montenegrin stitch, as well as Montenegrin stitch, was used during the seventeenth century in much the same way that cross stitch is used today. This stitch was used as an outline for design areas, and was also used as a filling stitch in these same areas. Samplers from this period have an almost reversible look, due in part to the use of this stitch.

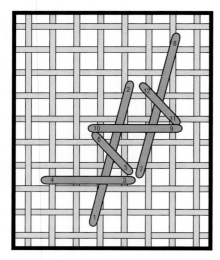

Illustration A

### Start
Use an away waste knot, version A, using the method described in Chapter 1.

### The Stitch
The diagonal Montenegrin stitch is composed of the three basic stitches used in the Montenegrin stitch. Although both stitches use the same format, a longer diagonal stitch (over six threads) is necessary to achieve the desired look on the back. See Illustrations A and B for diagonal Montenegrin stitch, version 1. See Illustrations C and D for diagonal Montenegrin stitch, version 2.

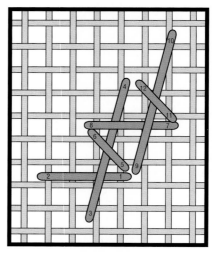

Illustration C

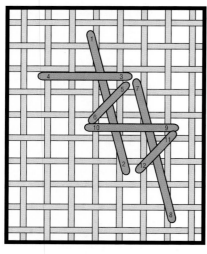

Illustration B

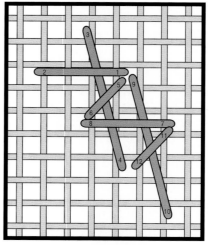

Illustration D

## The Back

With both versions of this reversible stitch, the back has the appearance of a plus sign with a diagonal stitch in opposite upper and lower corners. See Illustration E.

## Changing Threads

Use the method described in Chapter 1. Threads may be changed on the front or back of the fabric.

## Ending Threads

Run the thread under the stitches on the front or back of the fabric.

## Turning Corners

Since the diagonal Montenegrin stitch can only be worked on the diagonal, most corners will turn from Montenegrin stitch onto diagonal Montenegrin stitch. A transition stitch is necessary to reach the appropriate area to start the diagonal Montenegrin stitch. The transition stitch usually takes the shape of a plus sign the height and width of four threads. See Illustration F, which illustrates this transition in stitches 17–18, 21–22, and again in stitches 53–54 and 56–57. For turning corners, follow Illustration F for version 1, and Illustrations G and H for version 2.

*Reproduction by permission of the Syndics of the Fitzwilliam Museum, Cambridge, England*

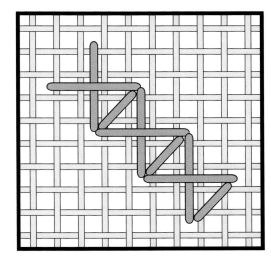

Illustration E

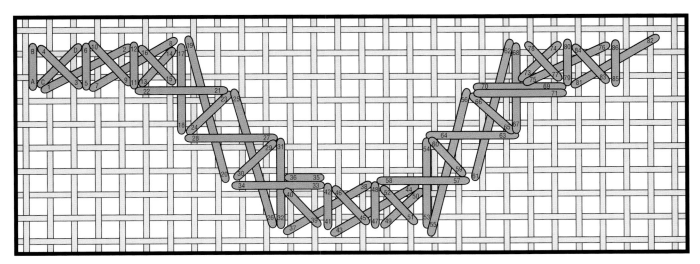

Illustration F

## Difficulties and Hints

This stitch should have a very dense back, giving the stitch a reversible quality. Because of the complicated nature of this stitch, check the back often to verify that all stitches are correctly located.

To determine the number of diagonal Montenegrin stitches required in a design, use a line drawn from the bottom corner of one square across the middle square and to the opposite corner of the third square, as seen in Illustration I. This line represents the long diagonal that is found in each of the diagonal Montenegrin stitches. Each line represents one diagonal Montenegrin stitch.

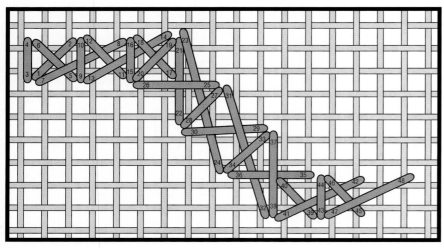

Illustration G

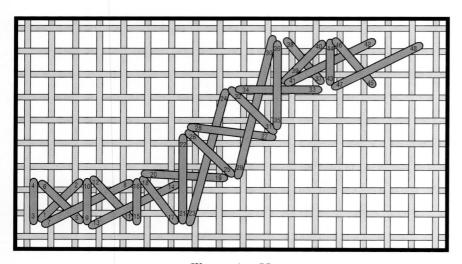

Illustration H

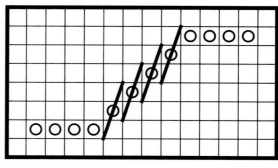

Illustration I

# Rice Stitch (William and Mary Stitch)

Rice stitch, an embellished cross stitch, has been popular since the sixteenth century. This stitch can be used as a border or for filling in a background.

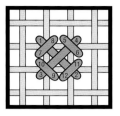

Illustration A

## Start
Use an away waste knot, version A or B, using the method described in Chapter 1.

## The Stitch
The stitch is constructed by working a cross stitch and, in a counterclockwise pattern, placing a diagonal backstitch on each arm of the cross stitch. A different texture is created by stitching the rice stitch over two threads (Illustration A) rather than over four threads (Illustration B).

## The Back
The back appears as vertical and horizontal stitches. See Illustration C.

## Changing Threads
Use the method described in Chapter 1.

## Ending Threads
Run the thread under the stitches on the back of the fabric.

## Turning Corners
When traveling distances or turning corners, run the thread under the stitches on the back of the fabric to reach the next stitch.

## Difficulties and Hints
Do not to stop in the middle of making this stitch, as the stitches are hard to distinguish one from another when many are worked in the same area. It is difficult to tell where one stitch stops and another begins. The rice stitch may be worked any size, from a regular cross stitch two threads by two threads, to a larger stitch, such as four threads by four threads. One color may be used for the base cross stitch, while another color may be used for the diagonals that cross each arm. See Illustration D. A variety of thread textures can be used, such as pearl cotton (coton perlé) for the base cross stitch with stranded cotton for the stitches that cross each arm. When using a combination of colors or threads, complete all base stitches first; then add diagonal stitches.

Illustration B

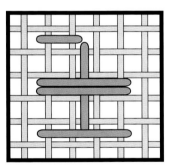

Illustration C

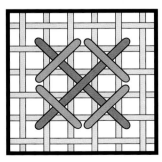

Illustration D

# Diagonal Rice Stitch

Diagonal rice stitch can be found in samplers that date to the seventeenth century. The stitch is similar to the rice stitch, with the following exception: where there are diagonals in rice stitch, there are straight stitches in diagonal rice stitch.

Illustration A

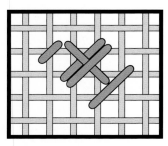

Illustration B

Illustration C

### Start
Use an away waste knot, version A or B, using the method described in Chapter 1.

### The Stitch
Begin this stitch with a vertical stitch over four threads. Center a horizontal stitch over four threads on top of the vertical stitch. Continue placing straight stitches in a counterclockwise pattern on top of the vertical and horizontal threads. See Illustration A.

### The Back
The back appears as diagonal stitches. See Illustration B.

### Changing Threads
Use the method described in Chapter 1.

### Ending Threads
Run the thread under the stitches on the back of the fabric.

### Turning Corners
When traveling distances or turning corners, run the thread under the stitches on the back of the fabric to reach the next stitch.

### Difficulties and Hints
Do not stop in the middle of making this stitch, as the stitches are hard to distinguish one from another when many are worked in the same area. It is difficult to tell where one stitch stops and another begins. See Illustration C. The diagonal rice stitch cannot be smaller than four threads by four threads but may be larger, if desired. One color can be used for the base cross stitch, while another color can be used for the straight stitches that cross each arm. A variety of thread textures can be used, such as pearl cotton (coton perlé) for the base cross stitch with stranded cotton for the stitches that cross each arm. When using a combination of colors or threads, complete all base stitches first; then add straight stitches.

# Smyrna Cross Stitch

This stitch is a simple embellishment of the cross stitch. Smyrna cross stitch has a unique, bumpy texture that is useful as a filling stitch. This stitch can also be used to outline or create a border.

### Start
Use an away waste knot, version A or B, using the method described in Chapter 1.

### The Stitch
Work a cross stitch as the base of this stitch. Place a vertical stitch on top of the cross stitch, with a horizontal stitch centered on top of the vertical stitch. This placement aids the eye in traveling from side to side. See Illustrations A and B. If an up-and-down movement is desired, place the horizontal stitch on top of the cross stitch and place the vertical stitch last. See Illustration C.

### The Back
This is not a reversible stitch. Very little thread is found on the back of the fabric. See Illustration D.

### Changing Threads
Use the method described in Chapter 1.

### Ending Threads
Run the thread under the stitches on the back of the fabric.

### Turning Corners
When traveling distances or turning corners, run the thread under the stitches on the back to reach the next stitch.

### Difficulties and Hints
One color may be used for the base cross stitch with another color used for the vertical and horizontal stitches. See Illustration E. A variety of thread textures can be used, such as pearl cotton (coton perlé) for the base cross stitch with stranded cotton for the horizontal and vertical stitches. When using a combination of colors or threads, complete all base stitches first, then add layered vertical and horizontal stitches. The Smyrna cross stitch is found in various sizes, such as two threads by two threads or four threads by four threads. See Illustrations A and B.

Illustration A

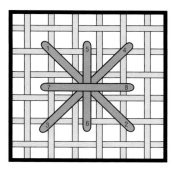

Illustration B

Illustration C

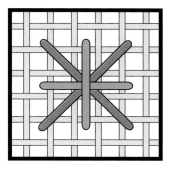

Illustration E

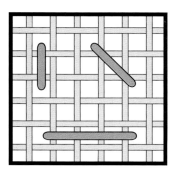

Illustration D

# Four-Sided Stitch

The four-sided stitch is a reversible stitch and is found in many types of embroidery. This stitch can be worked using normal tension, or using pulled tension for a lacy effect.

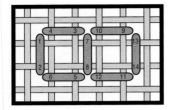

Illustration A

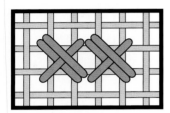

Illustration B

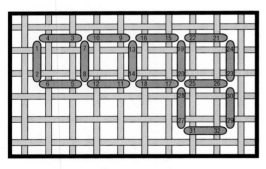

Illustration C

*Start*
Use an away waste knot, version A, using the method described in Chapter 1.

*The Stitch*
Four-sided stitch can be started on any of the four sides. Once the sequence of stitches is established, adhere to the order with every stitch. Four-sided stitch forms a square on the front of the fabric and a cross stitch on the back. There are straight stitches on the front of the fabric and diagonal stitches on the back of the fabric. (This information is useful when one is unable to determine which part of the stitch comes next.) Travel diagonally on the back of the fabric to the next stitch. See Illustration A for an example of the stitch sequence. Note that after the initial four sides of the first stitch are complete, the following stitches that lie side by side need only have three sides. Stitch 7–8 is a shared stitch with the next four-sided stitch.

*The Back*
The back of this reversible stitch appears as cross stitches with layered diagonal stitches. See Illustration B.

*Changing Threads*
Use the method described in Chapter 1.

*Ending Threads*
Run the thread under the stitches on the back of the fabric.

*Turning Corners*
Illustrations C, D, E, and F show the four corners possible using the four-sided stitch. Note the different sequence of stitches for each corner.

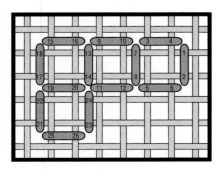

Illustration D

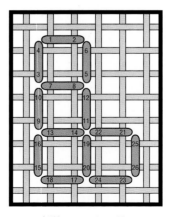

Illustration E

## Difficulties and Hints

This stitch can be used to form numbers and alphabets. The number 1, as seen in Illustration G, is given as an additional example of turning corners. In Illustration H, note that stitch 9–10 is placed to the right of the four-sided stitch rather than below the stitch, as seen in Illustration I. This choice creates a better appearance, due to the placement of the thread. The stitch pulls away from stitch 7–8, rather than across the opening where stitches 5, 8, 10, and 14 enter a common hole. See Illustration G.

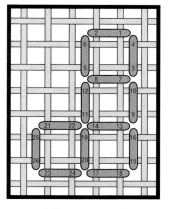

Illustration F

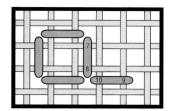

Illustration H

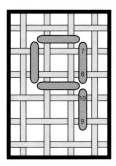

Illustration I

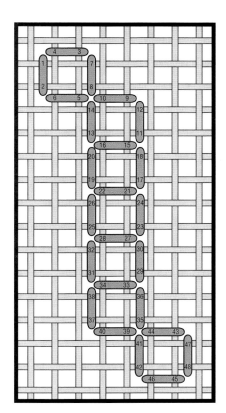

Illustration G

31

# Arrowhead Stitch (Double-Sided Italian Stitch)

Forms of arrowhead stitch have been found in samplers from the seventeenth century. This stitch is also known as double-sided Italian stitch. The technique creates a reversible stitch, which is also a pulled stitch.

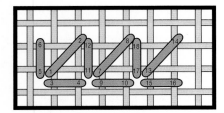

Illustration A

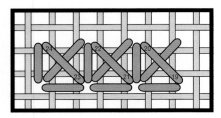

Illustration B

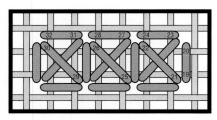

Illustration C

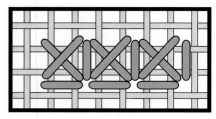

Illustration D

## Start
Use an away waste knot, version A, using the method described in Chapter 1.

## The Stitch
This stitch is created with two separate journeys of the thread. The first journey forms the three basic stitches that radiate out from the same hole. This gives the stitch the look of the head of an arrow. See Illustration A. The second journey crosses the diagonal stitches of the previous row, giving the appearance of a cross stitch. See Illustration B. The placement of optional compensation stitches—19–20, 23–24, 27–28, and 31–32—is shown in Illustration C. The compensation stitches create the appearance of a cross stitch inside a four-sided stitch. Pull tension on the odd stitches as the thread comes to the front of the fabric, creating small holes in each of the corners of the arrowhead stitch.

## The Back
The back of this reversible stitch appears the same as the front. See Illustration D.

## Changing Threads
Use the method described on Chapter 1. If necessary, the thread may be ended on the front of the fabric.

## Ending Threads
The thread may be ended on the front or back of the fabric, due to the denseness of this stitch.

## Turning Corners
This stitch is best executed in straight lines.

## Difficulties and Hints
Work the top row of the design area first, with subsequent rows placed below. After the first row is in place, the following rows do not require compensation stitches. The bottom of each succeeding row takes the place of compensation stitches.

When the second journey has been completed to carry the thread to the row below, conceal the thread behind the stitches already in place. This technique gives a more reversible appearance on the back of the fabric.

# Double Backstitch (Closed Herringbone)

Double backstitch is a very versatile, easily executed stitch that has the appearance of being plaited. Double backstitch can be used in straight lines, as an outline, on the diagonal, or in rows placed side by side as a filling stitch. The stitch name is derived from the appearance of the stitch back, which is twin, or double, rows of backstitch. Shadow work is another application for this stitch. See photo on page 46.

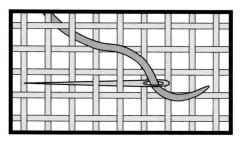

Illustration A

### Start
Use an away waste knot, version A, using the method described in Chapter 1.

### The Stitch
Double backstitch is best worked in a sewing motion. The needle is held in a horizontal position at all times while working this stitch. Bring the thread to the front of the fabric at 1, insert the needle into the fabric at 2, and bring the needle back to the front of the fabric at 3, working in one, continuous motion. See Illustration A. Repeat the same sewing motion two threads above, as shown in Illustration B. Repeat the sequence as necessary to complete the design, gathering the two threads of the fabric on the bottom of the stitch and then two threads of the fabric directly above. See Illustrations C and D.

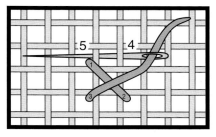

Illustration B

### The Back
The back of this reversible stitch appears as two horizontal rows of backstitch. See Illustration E. A double horizontal stitch in the same location can be seen where the thread ends or changes.

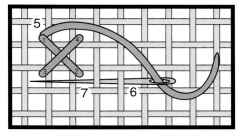

Illustration C

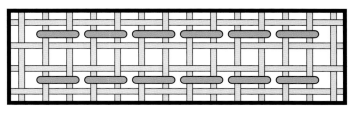

Illustration E

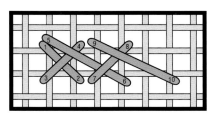

Illustration D

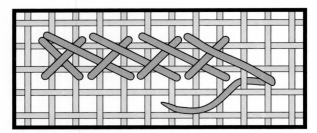

Illustration F

**Changing Threads**

Use the last stitch with the old thread to gather the two threads on the bottom of the fabric. See Illustration F. Bring the old thread to the front of the fabric, and leave it hanging out of the way of the stitching. Run the new thread under the existing stitches on the front of the fabric, repeating the last stitch taken with the old thread. See Illustration G. Continue stitching with the new thread in the same manner as before. See Illustration H. At the end of the new thread, thread the needle with the old thread and run the thread under the new stitches on the front of the fabric. See Illustration I.

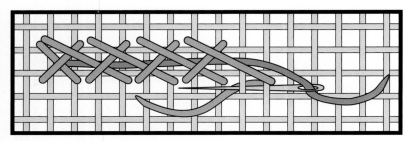

Illustration G

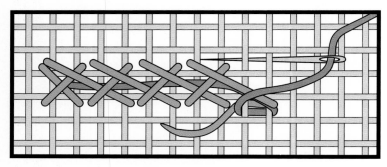

Illustration H

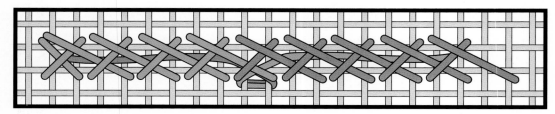

Illustration I

### Ending Threads

Work a compensation stitch to end the row of stitches. A compensation stitch is shown in Illustration J, and is numbered stitch 17–18. Bring the thread to the front of the fabric two threads to the left at 15. Run the thread under four or five existing stitches on the front of the fabric to secure. The away waste knot is ended in a similar manner by bringing the thread to the front of the fabric at 4 and running the thread under the existing stitches. See Illustration K.

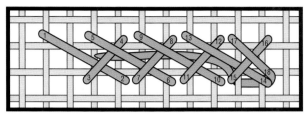

Illustration J

### Turning Corners

Illustration L shows the method required for turning an outside and an inside corner. After making stitch 14–15, turn the fabric 90° to continue stitching in a horizontal fashion.

### Difficulties and Hints

This stitch is a favorite because it is so problem-free. Be aware that to end the stitch in the described manner, the thickness of the stitches on the front of the fabric must be sufficient to hide the ending threads. Otherwise, end the threads on the back of the fabric by whipstitching along one of the back, horizontal lines. The stitch height and width may vary to accommodate different situations.

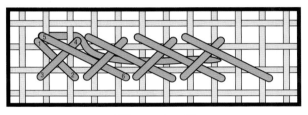

Illustration K

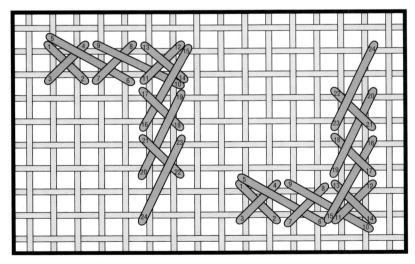

Illustration L

# Double-Backstitch Variation

Double backstitch variation is worked in the same manner as double backstitch, with the addition of a vertical stitch. This stitch results in the formation of squares on the fabric back, and gives a different appearance from the solid design on the front. Double backstitch variation can be used as a single border, an outline, or a filling stitch.

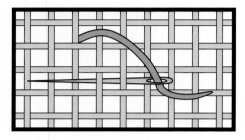

Illustration A

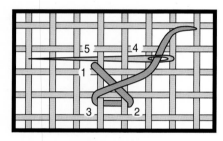

Illustration B

*Start*
Use an away waste knot, version A, using the method described in Chapter 1.

*The Stitch*
This stitch is executed in the same manner as double backstitch, with the addition of a vertical stitch placed on the left side of each double backstitch. The needle's position follows a pattern that places a horizontal stitch on the bottom (see Illustration A), a horizontal stitch on the top (see Illustration B), and a vertical stitch that enters the fabric in the lower-left corner of the stitch and exits the fabric from the upper-left corner of the stitch. See Illustration C. Repeated the sequence as necessary to complete the design. Note: Do not omit the vertical stitch at point 11–12. See Illustrations D and E.

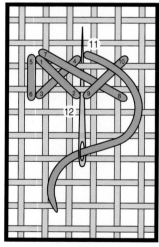

Illustration D

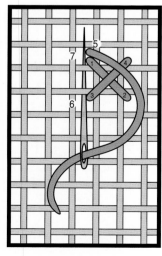

Illustration C

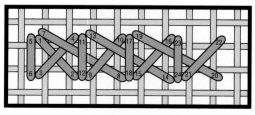

Illustration E

## The Back
The back of this reversible stitch appears as a row of squares. See Illustration F.

## Changing Threads
Use the same technique as for double backstitch.

## Ending Threads
End the threads using the same technique as for double backstitch. An additional vertical stitch may be placed at the end of the row to give the stitch a more complete look on the front, as well as on the back. Referring to Illustration G, bring the thread to the front at 29 and run the thread under the stitches on the front of the fabric. Note stitch 25–26 is a compensation stitch that will end the row of stitches. Stitch 27–28 is the compensation stitch that is placed to finish the stitched area.

## Turning Corners
The technique used for turning corners is the same as that used for double backstitch, with the exception of stitch 21–22, which is the horizontal stitch found on inside and outside corners. See Illustrations H and I. After completing stitch 21–22, turn the fabric 90° and bring the needle up at 23 to continue the double-backstitch variation in a horizontal position.

## Difficulties and Hints
Although this stitch is not difficult to execute, it is quite dense and, therefore, harder to see individual stitches on the fabric front. Check the back frequently as this will give the first indication of a missed stitch or problem. Double-backstitch variation may be worked on the diagonal, as seen in Illustration J. Stitches 19–20 and 21–22 show compensation stitches used to end the row.

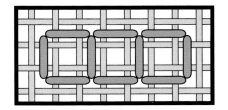

Illustration F

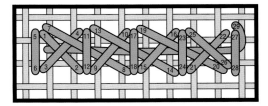

Illustration G

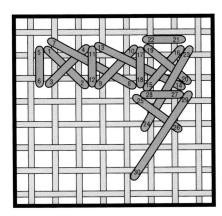

Illustration H

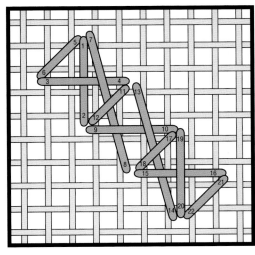

Illustration J

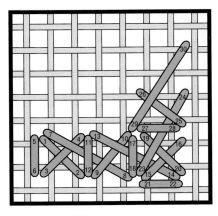

Illustration I

# Alternating Double Backstitch

Alternating double backstitch is primarily used as a border or a straight dividing line between borders. The stitch technique creates a chain effect. The number of stitches worked in each section of alternating double backstitch can vary; however, groups of three, representative of the Trinity, were most commonly used during the seventeenth century. This stitch is reversible.

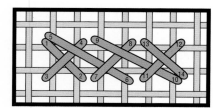

Illustration A (front)

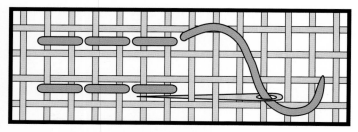

Illustration B  (back)

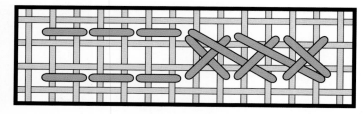

Illustration C  (back)

*Start*
Use an away waste knot, version A, using the method described in Chapter 1.

*The Stitch*
Begin this stitch in the same manner as the double backstitch. Work three double backstitches on the front of the fabric, bringing the thread to the back at 14. See Illustration A. Turn the fabric right-side down with the thread coming out the upper-right corner (on the back). See Illustration B. Repeat the sequence of stitches shown in Illustration A on the back of the fabric. See Illustration C. Turn fabric right-side up and repeat the sequence of stitches shown in Illustration A. Repeat the sequence as necessary to complete the design. To work alternating double backstitch by stitching only on the fabric front, follow the stitch sequence shown in Illustration D. Illustration E shows a series of sections of alternating double backstitch.

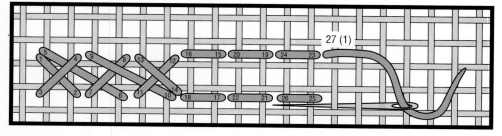

Illustration D  (front)

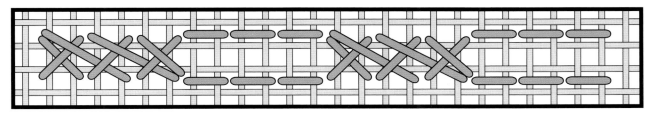

Illustration E (front)

## The Back

The back of this reversible stitch appears the same as the front, with alternating placement of the stitch groups. Where solid stitches appear on the fabric front, backstitches appear on the fabric back. Where backstitches appear on the fabric front, solid stitches appear on the fabric back. See Illustration F.

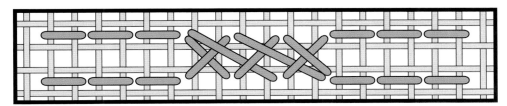

Illustration F (back)

## Changing Threads

Change the threads in the same manner as for double backstitch. Bring the thread from the front of the fabric to the back, carrying the thread under the solid areas of stitching. See Illustration G.

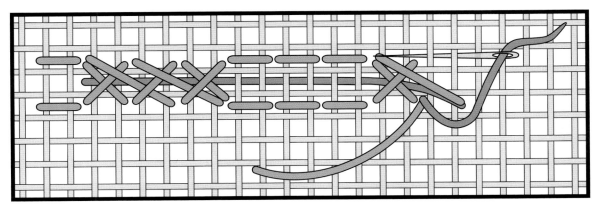

Illustration G (front)

## Ending Threads

Run the thread under the solid areas of stitches on the fabric front, just as in "Changing Threads". Illustration H shows the end compensation stitch and ending thread.

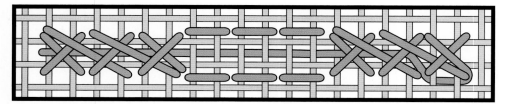

Illustration H (front)

## Turning Corners

Use the techniques described for double backstitch.

## Difficulties and Hints

When it is possible, turn the fabric when working this stitch. When it is not convenient to turn the fabric (i.e. when working in a frame), stitch only on the front of the fabric, following the stitch sequence shown in Illustration D.

*Reproduction by permission of the Syndics of the Fitzwilliam Museum, Cambridge, England*

40

# Williamsburg Stitch

Williamsburg stitch is worked in the same manner as double backstitch, with the addition of a diagonal stitch. The additional stitch is usually worked in a contrasting color to add decoration to the front and back of the fabric. A square stitch (as seen in double-backstitch variation) is formed with the second-color vertical stitches on the back of the fabric. Although this stitch may be used in any of the ways double backstitch is used, the author has only seen this technique in straight-line stitching.

This stitch was named Williamsburg stitch because it was first found on a seventeenth-century sampler in the collection at the DeWitt Wallace Decorative Arts Gallery in Williamsburg, Virginia.

*Start*
Use an away waste knot, version A, using the method described in Chapter 1.

*The Stitch*
Williamsburg stitch is constructed from a base stitch of double backstitch. See Illustration A. In a second journey, a diagonal stitch is placed on top of the double backstitch going from the upper-left corner to the lower-right corner of the stitch. See Illustration B.

*The Back*
The back of this reversible stitch appears as squares. If two thread colors are used, all horizontal stitches will appear in the color of the base stitch and all vertical stitches will appear in a contrasting color. See Illustration C.

*Changing Threads*
Bring the thread to the front of the fabric. See Illustration D. Place the new thread between the existing stitches and the front of the fabric, going down at point A and coming up at point B. See Illustration E. Using the new thread, repeat the last stitch taken with the old thread on the fabric back. Continue stitching using the new thread. Upon completion of the new thread, thread the needle using the old thread; run this thread under stitches worked using the new thread. See Illustration F.

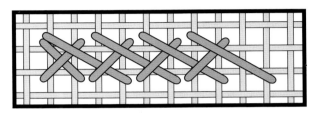

Illustration A

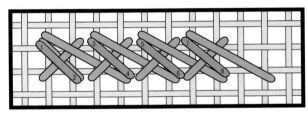

Illustration B

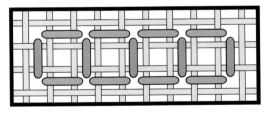

Illustration C

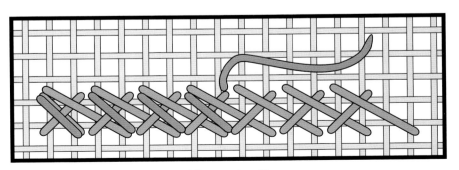

Illustration D

41

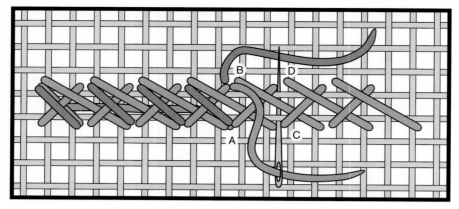

Illustration E

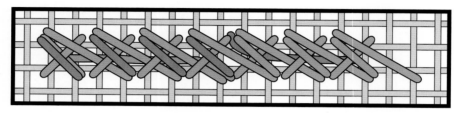

Illustration F

### Ending Threads

Bring the away-waste-knot thread from 1 vertically down on the fabric back, coming to the front in the lower-right corner of the first stitch. See Illustration G, point A. Run the thread under the stitches on the fabric front. The other end of the row of stitches will end in a similar manner; take the stitch vertically up on the fabric back, and bring the thread to the fabric front in the upper-right corner of the last stitch. Run the thread under the stitches on the front of the fabric.

### Turning Corners

Use the technique described for double backstitch.

### Difficulties and Hints

To give added decoration, the slant of the diagonal may be changed to go from lower left to upper right, even in the same line of stitches. See Illustration H.

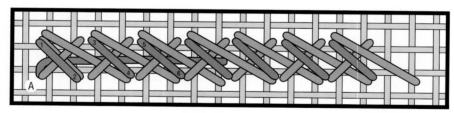

Illustration G

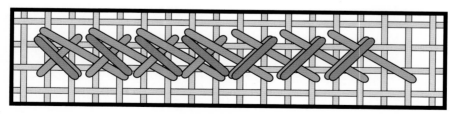

Illustration H

# Diagonal Double Backstitch

Diagonal double backstitch was often used during the seventeenth century for stitching the inside portions of vines. This stitch can be used alone or in combination with other stitches. Diagonal double backstitch can be used as an outline stitch and works well with other diagonal stitches, such as diagonal cross stitch or queen stitch.

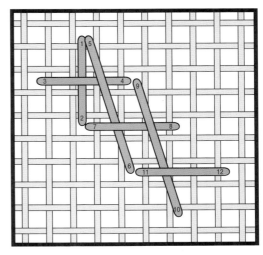

Illustration A

*Start*
Use an away waste knot, version A, using the method described in Chapter 1.

*The Stitch*
This stitch is best worked using a sewing motion just as double backstitch is worked; however, all the stitches are worked on the diagonal. Diagonal double backstitch can be worked over two threads or over four threads. See Illustrations A and B. Either method may be used. The method shown in Illustration B is more technically accurate, but it may be necessary to follow Illustration A in some instances, for filling in-between areas.

*The Back*
The back of this reversible stitch appears as double rows of diagonal backstitches. See Illustrations C and D.

*Changing Threads*
Use the technique described for double backstitch.

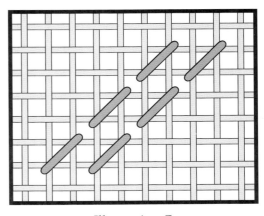

Illustration B

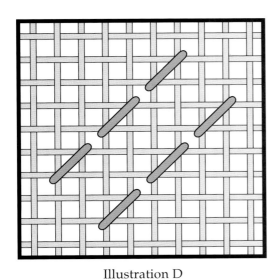

Illustration D

Illustration C

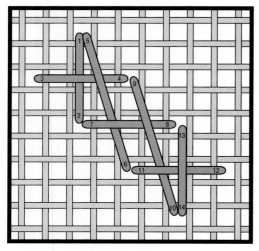

Illustration E

### Ending Threads

Use the technique described for double backstitch. Illustration E shows the beginning and ending of a diagonal line. Note the vertical stitch used as a compensation stitch at the beginning and end of the row.

### Turning Corners

Illustrations F, G, H, and I show methods used for turning corners. Diagonal double backstitch worked over two threads results in a narrow line of stitching. See Illustrations F and G. The same stitch worked over four threads results in a wider line of stitching. See Illustrations H and I. These illustrations show the method used to work from double backstitch to diagonal double backstitch and back to double backstitch. It may be necessary to change the direction of the carry-over thread to be consistent with the stitch sequence.

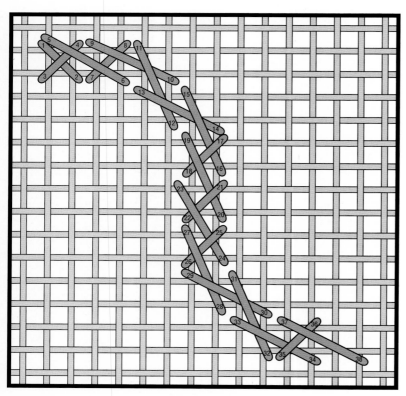

Illustration F

44

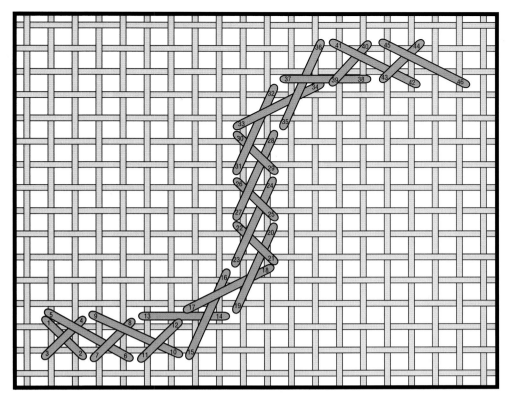

Illustration G

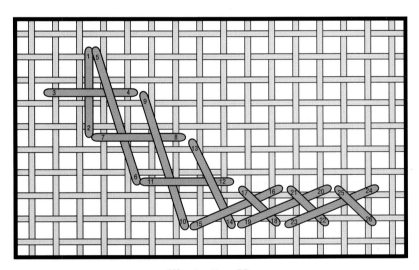

Illustration H

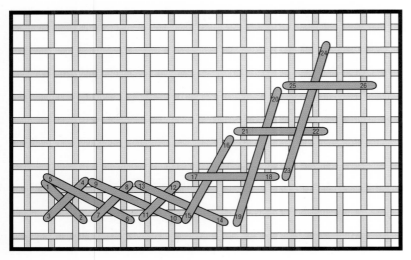

Illustration I

### Difficulties and Hints
The most difficult aspect of this stitch is turning corners. Remember to check the back often to make sure the double rows of backstitches are even on the corners. See Illustration J.

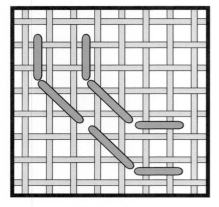

Illustration J

*Reproduction by permission of the Syndics of the Fitzwilliam Museum, Cambridge, England*

# Long-Arm Cross Stitch (Long-Leg Cross Stitch)

Long-arm cross stitch, like double backstitch, has the appearance of being braided. This stitch is most often used as a straight row of stitches or as a back filling stitch in Assisi work. This stitch is also called long-leg cross stitch.

### Start
Use an away waste knot, version A, using the method described in Chapter 1.

### The Stitch
Long-arm cross stitch is worked with only vertical motions of the needle. Insert the needle in the fabric at the bottom of the stitch. Count up two threads and bring the needle out of the fabric directly above. See Illustration A. Count two threads to the left and repeat the "in at the bottom, out at the top" motion as shown in Illustration B. Next, count two threads to the right beyond the existing stitch and again use the sewing motion "in at the bottom, out at the top." See Illustration C. Finish the stitch by moving two threads to the left and completing the sewing motion. See Illustration D. Continue in this manner for the desired number of stitches.

### The Back
The back of this reversible stitch appears as vertical lines spaced every two threads. See Illustration E.

### Changing Threads
The method used for changing threads is similar to that used for double backstitch. Bring the thread to the front of the fabric. Run the new thread under the stitches on the front of the fabric. Repeat the last stitch taken with the

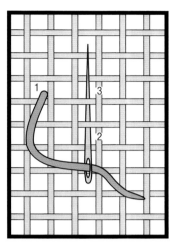

Illustration A

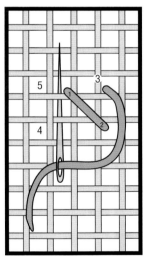

Illustration B

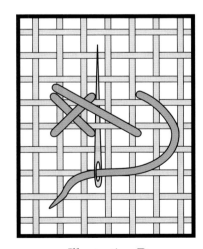

Illustration D

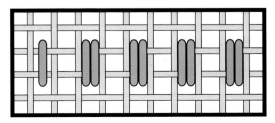

Illustration E

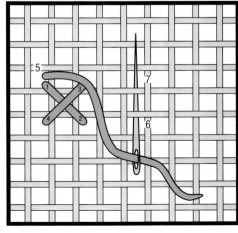

Illustration C

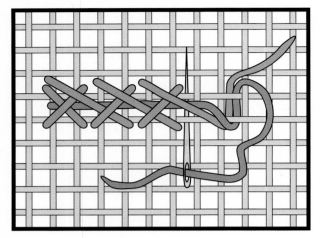

Illustration F

old thread. See Illustrations F and G. Continue stitching in the same manner as before.

### Ending Threads
End the thread at the end of a row by taking a compensation stitch from the upper-left corner to the lower-right corner of the last long-arm cross stitch. Bring the thread out in the upper-right corner and run the thread under the stitches on the front of the fabric. See Illustration H. Clip the thread close to the stitches so that the thread ends will spring back and be hidden under the stitches.

### Turning Corners
Illustrations I and J show the method required for turning an outside and an inside corner, respectively. After taking stitch 14–15, turn the fabric 90° to continue stitching in a horizontal fashion.

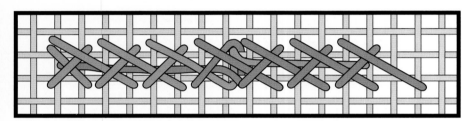

Illustration G

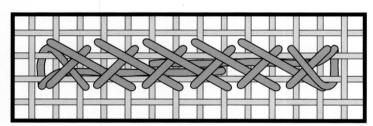

Illustration H

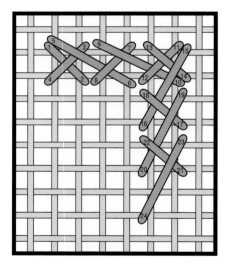

Illustration I

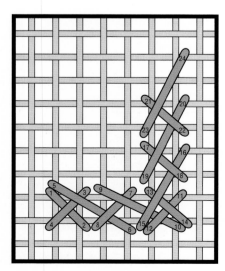

Illustration J

### Difficulties and Hints
To be able to end the stitch in the described manner, the thickness of the stitches on the front of the fabric must be sufficient to hide the ending threads. Otherwise, end the threads by running them under the stitches on the back of the fabric. If several rows of long-arm cross stitch are in place, such as a background filling, it is possible to whipstitch along the vertical lines formed on the back.

48

# Herringbone Stitch

Herringbone stitch has remained popular through the years, perhaps due to the ease of stitching and its light and airy decorative, zigzag effect. This stitch has the appearance of the top view of a split-rail fence. Herringbone stitches have appeared in antique samplers as bands that divide rows of patterns.

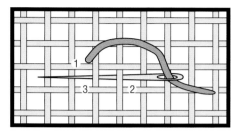

Illustration A

### Start
Use an away waste knot, version A, using the method described in Chapter 1.

### The Stitch
This stitch is worked with horizontal motions of the needle. The stitches are staggered, creating an open, lacy effect. Begin with compensation stitch 1–2 to give a look of completion to the row of stitches. Gather stitch 2–3 in the needle and pull the thread through. See Illustration A. Carry the thread up two threads and over four threads of the fabric and repeat the same horizontal motion with stitch 4–5. See Illustration B. Note that 5 is two threads above 2. Continue stitching in a zigzag manner. See Illustration C.

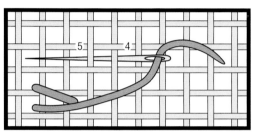

Illustration B

### The Back
Herringbone stitch has very few stitches on the back. The majority of the thread remains on the front of the fabric. The stitches on the back of the fabric will be staggered. See Illustration D.

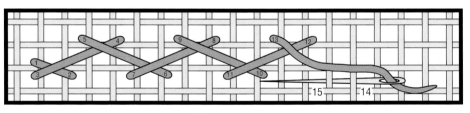

Illustration C

### Changing Threads
Bring the old thread to the front of the fabric, and leave it hanging out of the way of the stitching. Start the new thread with another away waste knot for ease of anchoring the thread later on. See Illustration E.

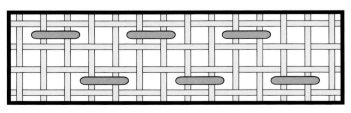

Illustration D

Illustration E

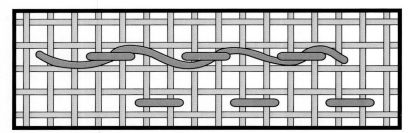

Illustration F

### Ending Threads

A compensation stitch, such as stitch 1–2 in Illustration C, is necessary to give a finished appearance. To anchor the thread ends, whipstitch around the existing stitches in a horizontal line on the back of the fabric. See Illustration F.

### Turning Corners

Use the technique described for double backstitch.

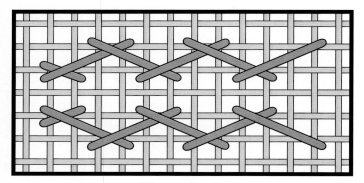

Illustration G

### Difficulties and Hints

Although ending the thread is not difficult, it seems to be a disadvantage of the stitch. Make sure herringbone stitches are staggered. The edges of the stitches should be directly above one another. See 2 and 5 or 4 and 7 in Illustration C. Illustrations G and H show different compensation stitches.

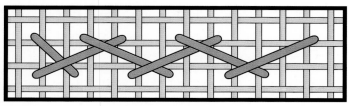

Illustration H

50

# Double Herringbone Stitch

Double herringbone stitch is a variation of the herringbone stitch. The technique uses two contrasting colors and is best used as a decorative border.

*Start*
Use an away waste knot, version A, using the method described in Chapter 1.

*The Stitch*
The stitch consists of two rows of herringbone stitch in contrasting colors, worked one on top of the other, interlacing the diagonal threads. See Illustration A. The numerals refer to the first journey and the letters designate the second journey of the double herringbone stitch. See Illustration B.

*The Back*
The back appears as two rows of backstitch in alternating colors. See Illustration C.

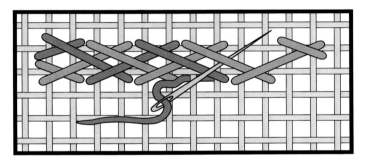

Illustration A

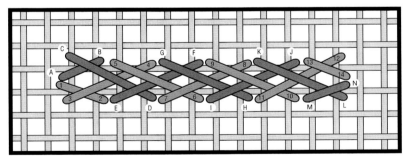

Illustration B

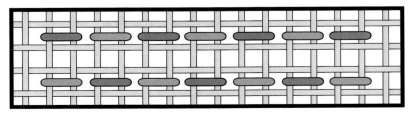

Illustration C

51

## Changing Threads

If the thread is to be changed on the first row of herringbone stitch, do not anchor the old thread. Bring the thread to the front of the fabric and leave it hanging out of the way of the stitching. End threads only after both journeys of the double herringbone stitch have been completed. Using an away waste knot, bring the new thread up in the same location where the old thread was brought to the front of the fabric. See Illustration D. Continue stitching in the same manner as before. After the base row of herringbone stitch has been completed, begin filling in the empty spaces of the herringbone stitch with another row, using a contrasting thread color. After completing both rows of herringbone stitch, end all threads.

Illustration D

## Ending Threads

Run the thread under the stitches on the front of the fabric only after both journeys are complete. See Illustration E. Follow Illustration B for adding compensation stitches at the beginning and end of each row.

## Turning Corners

Turning corners is not applicable to this stitch.

## Difficulties and Hints

Do not change both thread colors in the same location, as several thread ends cause bulkiness.

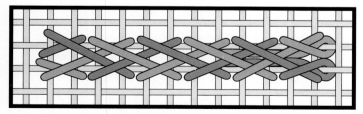

Illustration E

# Chapter Three

# *Buttonhole Stitch Family*

All the stitches in this chapter are worked using a thread loop, or a buttonhole base. The
close, binding edge of buttonhole stitch makes
this stitch a good choice for finishing raw edges,
especially in those areas where cutwork is included on embroidery pieces. Buttonhole stitch
was used in needlework from the 1600s and
1700s to create simple lines, as well as incorpo-
rate scalloped edges and borders of elements
within a sampler design. Buttonhole stitch is
worked in a loop stitch that covers both the
front and the back of the fabric with thread. The
four related stitches—buttonhole bar stitch, detached buttonhole stitch, hollie-point stitch, and
trellis stitch—are worked primarily on the front
of the fabric, with little thread on the back of
the fabric. The techniques used to create these
stitches give added texture to stitchery. Although trellis stitch gives the appearance of a
looped stitch, it is created using a series of knots.

# Buttonhole Stitch

Buttonhole stitch is used in many forms of cutwork. This stitch works well for securing raw edges, and can also be used to work borders, scalloped edges, and a simple line of stitching. The looped edge on the bottom of the stitch gives a finished look.

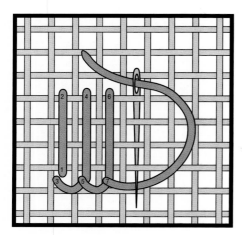

Illustration A

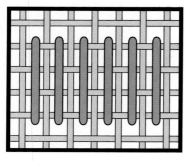

Illustration B

*Start*
Use an away waste knot, version A, using the method described in Chapter 1.

*The Stitch*
Buttonhole stitch is a satin stitch that catches on the loop of thread at the bottom of the stitch. This forms a tight row of loops at the bottom of the stitch. See Illustration A.

*The Back*
The back of the stitch appears as vertical stitches. See Illustration B.

*Changing Threads*
Bring the thread to the front of the fabric and leave it hanging out of the way of the stitching. See Illustration C. Run the new thread under the existing stitches on the back of the fabric, bringing the thread to the front of the fabric in the same hole as the old thread. See Illustration D. Continue working the buttonhole stitch as illustrated. End the old thread by taking it back through the hole from which it came and run the thread under the new stitches. When two areas of buttonhole stitch need to be connected, take the thread from the bottom loop of the last stitch worked and carry this thread across into the bottom loop of the section being connected. See Illustration E.

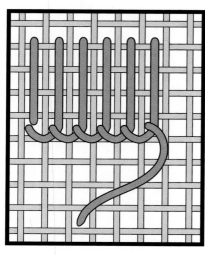

Illustration C

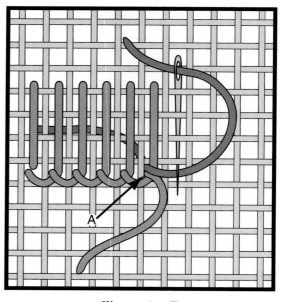

Illustration D

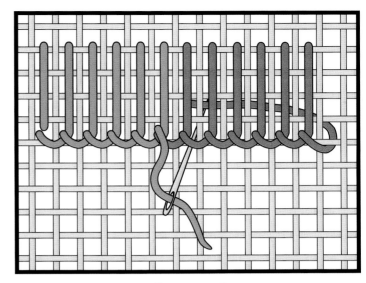

Illustration E

### Ending Threads

Carry the looped thread at the bottom of the stitch over the fabric thread to the right and the run the thread under the stitches on the back of the fabric. See Illustration F.

### Turning Corners

The method used for turning corners with the buttonhole stitch is similar to that used with the satin stitch. Illustration G shows the buttonhole wheel, a stitch variation found on many seventeenth-century samplers. Continual turning of the fabric is required to complete this technique. See Illustrations H and I for additional techniques used for turning corners. Illustration I can be used in conjunction with Hardanger embroidery to work a buttonhole edging that is used to bind cut edgings.

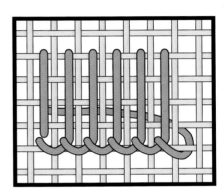

Illustration F

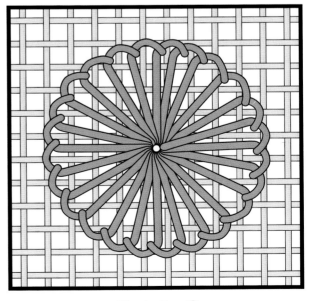

Illustration G

55

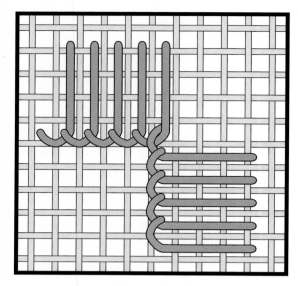

Illustration H

### Difficulties and Hints

Starting this stitch is the most difficult part. The loop is held to the left as the beginning stitch is worked. See Illustration J. This creates the illusion that the stitch has the same tight loop at the bottom as the other stitches. Pull the thread through the fabric as far as possible before releasing the thread held under the thumb. Illustration K shows alternate placement of thread for beginning this stitch.

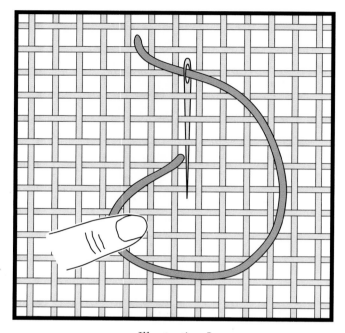

Illustration J

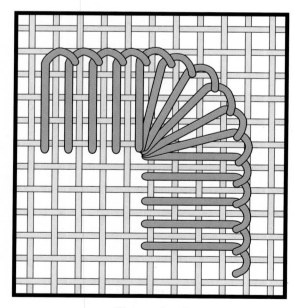

Illustration I

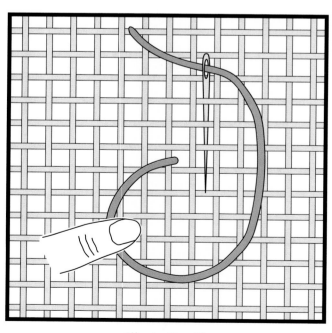

Illustration K

56

# Buttonhole-Bar Stitch

Buttonhole-bar stitch is used as a decorative stitch. Its three-dimensional properties give it a unique appearance. This stitch may also be used for stabilizing bars spanning the open areas of cutwork. Buttonhole bars were popular in whitework samplers of the seventeenth century.

### Start
Use an away waste knot, version A, using the method described in Chapter 1.

### The Stitch
Buttonhole bars begin with three loops of thread placed over the number of fabric threads required for the length of the stitch. A buttonhole stitch is then worked over the three thread loops. Note that the buttonhole stitches do not enter the fabric. See Illustration A. Illustration B shows a completed section of the bar over seven threads. The buttonhole stitch worked over the three loops should fill the space without appearing crowded. Crowding may cause the loops to bow outward and some twisting may occur. See Illustration C. The placement of two buttonhole bars in the same location on the fabric is shown in Illustration C. Note that the looped edge remains on the outer edges of the stitches.

### The Back
The back appear as three loops of thread. See Illustration D.

### Changing Threads
Do not change threads in the middle of a buttonhole bar. Start a new thread on the next bar to be worked.

### Ending Threads
Loop the thread over the stitches on the back of the fabric. Knotting may be required to secure the thread.

### Turning Corners
This stitch is worked in straight units. To turn a corner, place the thread loops in the direction of travel. This can be horizontal, vertical, or diagonal.

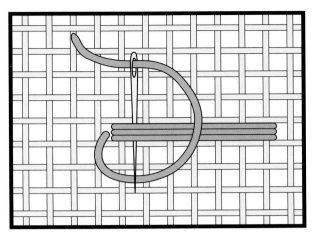

Illustration A

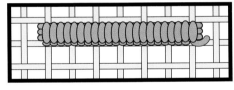

Illustration B

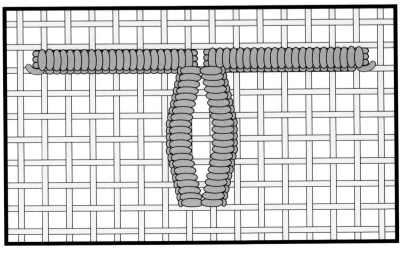

Illustration C

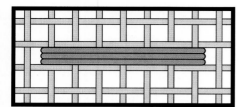

Illustration D

### Difficulties and Hints

Note the number of buttonhole stitches required to cover the looped-thread bar. When stitching more than one buttonhole bar of the same length, use the same number of buttonhole stitches for each bar. Using too many buttonhole stitches will cause the bar to twist. This can be a desired effect, since this adds additional texture. The most difficult part of this technique is ending the stitch. Although there will be only three long threads on the fabric back, looping and knotting the thread around these threads may be the only way to effectively end the thread. See Illustration D. The formation of stitches in Illustration E lends itself well to flower designs and is presented here as an example of a use of the stitch.

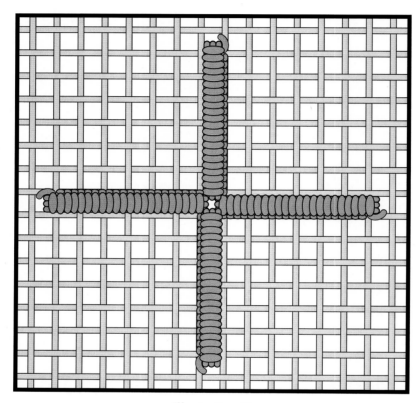

Illustration E

58

# Detached Buttonhole Stitch

Detached buttonhole stitch was a favored stitch during the seventeenth century. This technique was used to embellish clothing, as a filling stitch for the petals of flowers, or for applications where solid coverage was desired. This stitch can be used to fill in odd-shaped areas with ease. Shading is easy to achieve with this stitch.

### Start
Use an away waste knot, version A, using the method described in Chapter 1.

### The Stitch
Detached buttonhole with trailing thread:
Outline the area to be worked, using backstitch or double running stitch. Work this so that the stitches end in the upper right-hand corner of the design area (point A). Next, come up in the center of stitch A and place a trailing thread, stitch B–C, across the design area. Bring the thread up at point D to start the buttonhole stitches. See Illustration A.

Detached buttonhole is worked on top of the fabric, never entering the fabric until the stitch is complete. Illustration A shows the position of the needle going under the backstitch (or double running stitch), under the trailing thread, and over the loop of the thread. This sequence constructs the buttonhole stitch. Repeat this sequence to work one buttonhole stitch for each backstitch until the row is complete. If a smoother appearance is desired, add more buttonhole stitches for each backstitch. At the end of the row, carry the thread to the back of the fabric at point E. Refer to Illustration B to start the next row. Bring the thread to the front of the fabric in the center of the next backstitch at point F. Place another trailing thread

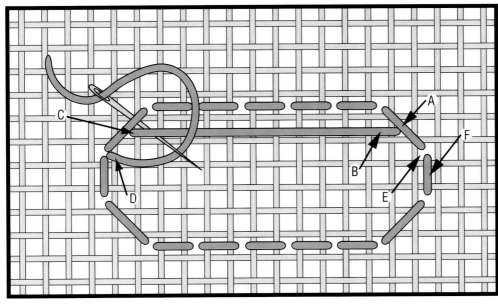

Illustration A

across the design area and continue the sequence as before. See Illustration B. The needle will go under the bottom loop of the buttonhole stitch of the previous row, under the trailing thread, and then over the loop. Repeat these steps until all rows are finished except the last row of the design area. This row is worked with a slight variation. See Illustration C. To anchor the design on the last row, the needle is placed under the buttonhole loop, the trailing thread, and the backstitch (or double running stitch), and over the loop.

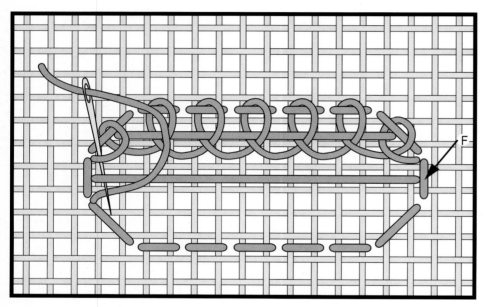

Illustration B

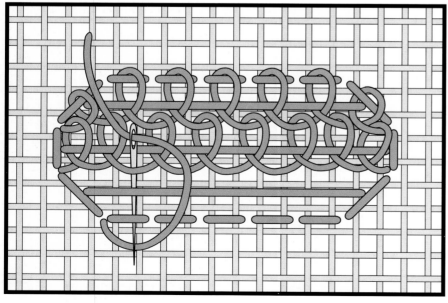

Illlustration C

Detached Buttonhole without trailing thread:
Outline the design area with backstitch or double running stitch. Work this so that the stitches end in the upper
right-hand corner of the design area (point A). Bring the
thread to the front of the fabric at point A. See Illustration
D. Work buttonhole stitches by sliding the needle under
the backstitch and over the loop of the thread. Keep the
tension even so that the rows do not arch in the center.
Repeat this sequence to work one buttonhole stitch for
each backstitch until the row is complete. At the end of
the row, carry the thread to the back at point B and bring
the thread to the front of the fabric in the center of the
next backstitch at point C. See Illustration D. Work the
stitch as before, traveling in the opposite direction. The
thread will go under the loop of the buttonhole stitch in
the previous row to connect the rows of buttonhole
stitches. Each subsequent row places one buttonhole stitch
for each buttonhole stitch in the previous row. To anchor
the design on the last row, carry the thread under the buttonhole loop and the backstitch. This stitch is worked following the same method, whether worked diagonally, as
shown, or horizontally.

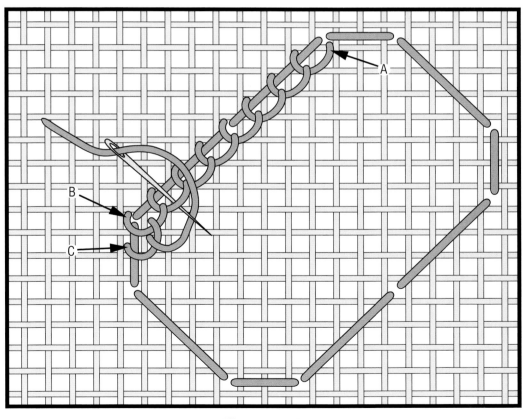

Illustration D

### The Back
The back of this reversible stitch appears as the stitch used for the outline (backstitch or double running stitch) in the shape of the design area.

### Changing Threads
Never change the thread in the middle of a row. Always end the thread in the previous row if there is insufficient thread to complete another row.

### Ending Threads
Run the thread under the stitches on the back of the fabric. If backstitch is used, run the thread around the stitches on the back of the fabric. If double running stitch is used for the outline, refer to the double running stitch for the method used.

### Turning Corners
Turning corners is not applicable to this stitch as the stitch follows the shape of the design area.

### Difficulties and Hints
The most difficult part of this stitch is keeping the correct tension. If too tight a tension is used, a slight curve or arch will occur in the center area of the row. Tight tension throughout the design area will result in distortion of the stitches. Try to keep the bottom of each row level with the bottom of the backstitch (or double running stitch) in the outline. Shading is easily accomplished with this stitch by changing the color with each row of stitches. For example, the first row could be dark, the middle row could be a medium color, and the bottom row could be a light color.

*Reproduction by permission of the Syndics of the Fitzwilliam Museum, Cambridge, England*

# Hollie-Point Stitch

Hollie-point stitch is considered a lace stitch and gives a delicate effect to needlework. This stitch was found in samplers of the seventeenth and eighteenth centuries, and by the mid-eighteenth century, small squares of this stitch were worked on samplers over cut-out areas of the fabric. These samplers were primarily whitework samplers.

### Start
Use an away waste knot, version A, using the method described in Chapter 1.

### The Stitch
Outline the area to be worked with a double running stitch. (Chain stitch can also be used.) Work this so that the stitches end in the upper-right corner of the design area. Bring the thread to the front of the fabric at point A, place a trailing thread, stitch B–C, across the design area, and carry the thread to the back of the fabric. See Illustration A. Bring the thread to the front of the fabric at point D. Wrap the thread around the thumb, right to left. Slip the needle under the double running stitch, under the trailing thread, and under the thread around the thumb. See Illustration A. Pull the thread until a knot is formed. Repeat the sequence to work the row. Work the next row in the same manner, except pass the needle under the loop of the previous row, under the trailing thread, and under the thread around the thumb. See Illustration B. To anchor the design on the last row, the needle is placed under the loop of the previous row, under the trailing thread, under the thumb loop, and under the double running stitch.

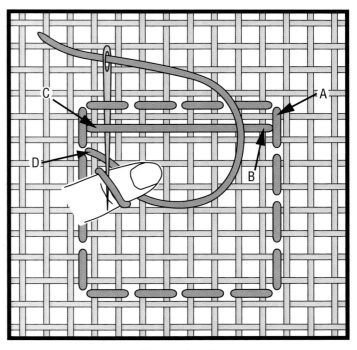

Illustration A

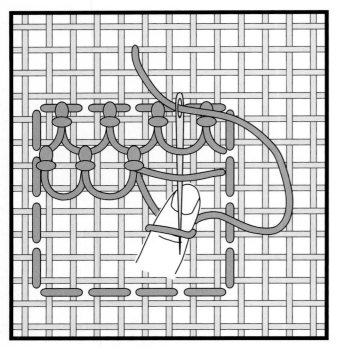

Illustration B

### The Back

The back of this reversible stitch appears as the stitch used for the outline (double running stitch or chain stitch) in the shape of the design area.

### Changing Threads

Never change the thread in the middle of a row. Always end the thread in the previous row if there is insufficient thread to complete another row.

### Ending Threads

Run the threads under the stitches on the back of the fabric. If a double running stitch is used for the outline, refer to the double running stitch for the method used. If a chain stitch is used, refer to the chain stitch for the method used.

### Turning Corners

Turning corners is not applicable to this stitch as the stitch follows the design area.

### Difficulties and Hints

The most difficult part of this stitch is keeping the correct tension. If too tight a tension is used, a slight curve or arch will occur in the center area of the row. Tight tension throughout the design area will result in distortion of the stitches. Try to keep the bottom of each row level with the bottom of the double running stitch in the outline. Shading is easily accomplished with this stitch by changing the color with each row of stitches. For example, the first row could be dark, the middle row could be a medium color, and the bottom row could be a light color.

*Reproduction by permission of the Syndics of the Fitzwilliam Museum, Cambridge, England*

# Trellis Stitch

Trellis stitch, similar in appearance to the detached buttonhole, is worked using an unusual technique that results in a much tighter effect. This stitch is best worked in straight rows. Trellis stitch was a very popular stitch used on samplers from the sixteenth and seventeenth centuries. It was used on clothing of those times as well. Trellis stitch is used to work solid areas and can adapt to many shapes, including circular patterns. This stitch works well in shading applications.

### Start
Use an away waste knot, version A, following the method describe in Chapter 1.

### The Stitch
Outline the perimeter of the design area using double running stitch or chain stitch, ending in the upper-left corner. See Illustration A. Bring the needle to the front of the fabric at point A. Slip the needle under the double running stitch along the top line of stitching at point B. Wrap the thread around in a loop back into itself, forming a knot when pulled. See Illustration B. Repeat this sequence across the row, ending into the center of the stitch at point C. See Illustration C. Bring the thread to the front of the fabric at point D to begin a new row and slip the needle under the thread between the knots. Form another loop and slip the knot into itself, as seen in Illustration D. Work the row in the opposite direction of the previous row. See Illustration E.

Anchor the last row of stitching into the bottom outline, referring to the method used for detached buttonhole stitch. Any irregularities in working this stitch will lead to an undesired effect. It is best to use flat silk thread or an untwisted thread for this stitch technique.

To create a pattern of parallel slanting lines, place all stitches in the same direction by carrying the thread under the back of the design area and working all rows from left to right.

### The Back
The back appears as the stitch used for the outline (double running stitch or chain stitch) in the shape of the design area.

### Changing Threads
Never change the thread in the middle of a row. Always end the thread in the previous row if there is insufficient thread to complete another row.

### Ending Threads
Run the threads under the stitches on the back of the fabric.

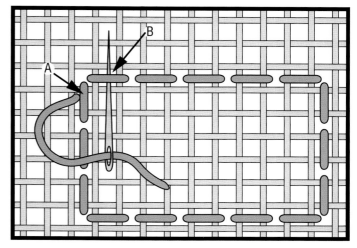

Illustration A

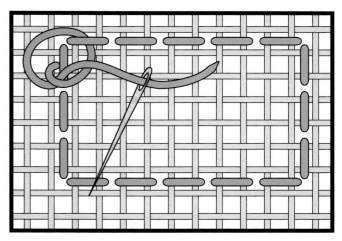

Illustration B

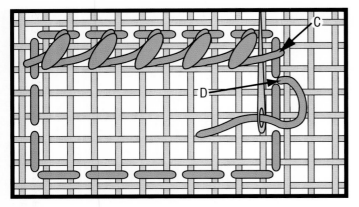

Illustration C

## Turning Corners
Turning corners is not applicable to this stitch as the stitch follows the shape of the design area.

## Difficulties and Hints
The most difficult part of this stitch is keeping the correct tension. If too tight a tension is used, a slight curve or arch will occur in the center area of the row. Tight tension throughout the design area will result in distortion of the stitches. Try to keep the bottom of each row level with the bottom of the double running stitch in the outline. Shading is easily accomplished with this stitch by changing the color with each row of stitches. For example, the first row could be dark, the middle row could be a medium color, and the bottom row could be a light color.

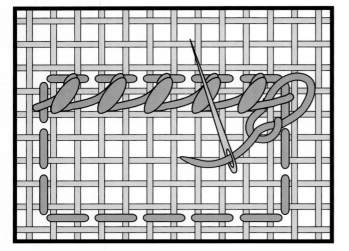

Illllustration D

*Reproduction by permission of the Syndics of the Fitzwilliam Museum, Cambridge, England*

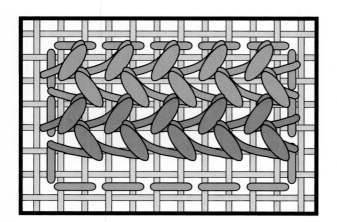

Illustration E

66

# Chapter Four
# Satin Stitch Family

All the stitches in this chapter are worked using straight stitches and have a smooth texture and appearance on the front of the fabric. The stitches are worked without using loops. Tent and Gobelin stitch have slanted placements, but otherwise have the same, smooth appearance. Algerian eye stitch and eyelet stitch are worked by repeatedly passing the needle through a common center point. The straight legs of the stitch are worked in a circular fashion. Algerian eye stitch was often used on samplers of the sixteenth and seventeenth centuries to form alphabet letters, borders, and geometric designs. This stitch was almost as popular as cross stitch for stitching alphabets in that period. Irish stitch is constructed by working parallel lines over varying numbers of threads, for a staggered effect, usually enhanced by the use of several shades of thread. Hungarian stitch and Parisian stitch are worked in similar fashion, with a group of vertical threads over two threads, then over four threads, then over two threads, in a diamond shape. Satin stitch, brick stitch, and kloster-block stitch are smooth-textured stitches created using straight stitches that cover four threads or more.

## Algerian Eye Stitch

Algerian eye stitch, worked primarily as a decorative stitch, produces a lace effect on the fabric. This is due to the construction of the stitch; numerous threads occupy a common hole in the center of the stitch. The center hole will vary in size, based on the amount of tension placed on the thread.

Illustration A

Illustration B

### Start
Use an away waste knot, version A, using the method described in Chapter 1.

### The Stitch
Begin this stitch on any of the four sides with a horizontal or vertical stitch rather than a diagonal stitch. Starting on the diagonal tends to pull the fabric threads more unevenly, resulting in a less-square appearance of the stitch. However, in some instances, starting on the horizontal or vertical may not be possible. Referring to Illustration A, carry the thread from the horizontal or vertical to the center common point and continue to work the stitch in a clockwise or counterclockwise method. The clockwise version is detailed in Illustration A. Illustration C shows the Algerian eye over four threads.

### The Back
The back of this reversible stitch appears the same as the front, with the exception of stitch 1–2. See Illustration B for the back view of the stitch worked over six threads. See Illustration D for the back view of the stitch worked over four threads.

Illustration C

Illustration D

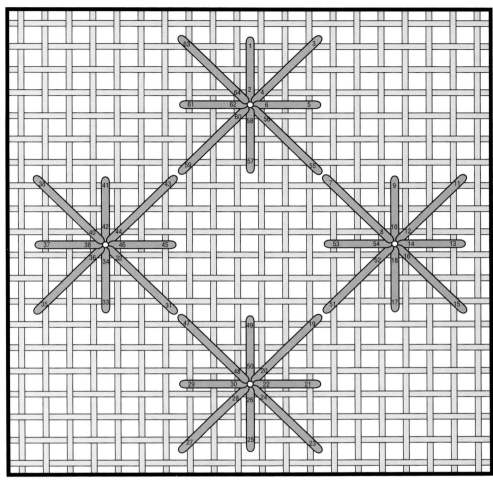

Illustration E

### Changing Threads
Use the method described in Chapter 1.

### Ending Threads
Run the thread under the stitches on the back of the fabric.

### Turning Corners
Illustration E shows a method for turning corners. Using this method will result in a reversible effect on the back of the fabric.

### Difficulties and Hints
When carrying the thread from one Algerian eye to the next, make sure that the thread is never carried across the open eye. Carry the thread under existing stitches on the back in order to avoid the center opening of the stitch.

# Eyelet Stitch

Eyelet stitch is similar to Algerian eye stitch in look and construction. However, eyelet is a stronger and heavier stitch than the lacy effect presented by Algerian eye. Eyelet stitch is used as a filling stitch. See photo on page 73.

Illustration A

Illustration B

Illustration C

Illustration D

### Start
Use an away waste knot, version A, using the method described in Chapter 1.

### The Stitch
Eyelet stitch is constructed in the same manner as the Algerian eye. The difference lies in the denseness of the stitch, or the number of threads used to complete the stitch. Unlike Algerian eye, eyelet places one stitch to the center hole for each thread of the fabric. See Illustration A. The tension can be varied to create different degrees of openness of the central eye of the stitch. Illustration C shows the stitch over four threads. Eyelets can also take various shapes. Illustrations E and F show the stitch worked in a diamond shape. Illustrations G and H are variations of the eyelet concept; note that the stitch does not have to have sharp corners or a specific shape. The use of different weights or colors of thread can add much interest to the technique. Two types of thread can be used, such as a silk thread used with a metallic thread. See Illustration I.

Another method of working the eyelet stitch is achieved by placing stitches between every other thread of the fabric in a clockwise pattern, and filling in the missing stitches on the return, counterclockwise journey. See Illustration J.

Illustration E

### The Back

The back of this reversible stitch appears the same as the front, with the exception of stitch 1. See Illustration B for the back view of the stitch worked over two threads. See Illustration D for the back view of the stitch worked over four threads.

### Changing Threads

Use the method described in Chapter 1.

### Ending Threads

Run the thread under the stitches on the back of the fabric.

### Turning Corners

Use the methods described for the Algerian eye. The thread can be run under stitches on the back of the fabric to the area of the next eyelet.

### Difficulties and Hints

Do not run the thread across the back of an open eye. When the eyelet is constructed from the outside of the stitch into the central hole, a sharp, clear look to the center hole is created. When a softer appearance to the central hole is desired, reverse the stitching order by coming up from the center and taking the stitches to the edge of the eyelet.

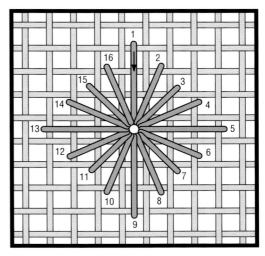

Illustration F

Illustration G

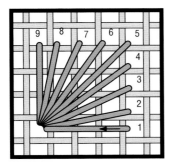

Illustration H

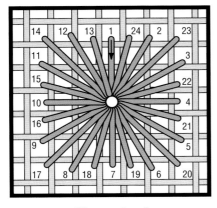

Illustration J

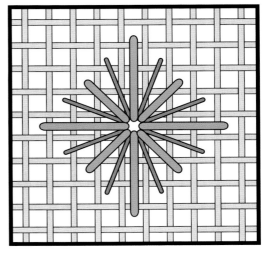

Illustration I

# Satin Stitch (Geometric Satin Stitch)

Satin stitch is a group of straight stitches placed side by side. The name is derived from the smooth texture created by the stitch. This stitch is primarily used as a filling stitch, although it can also be used as an outline stitch.

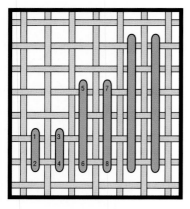

Illustration A

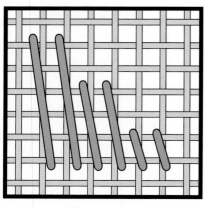

Illustration B

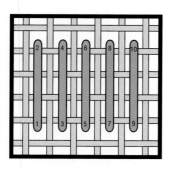

Illustration C

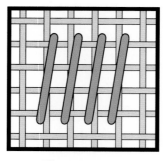

Illustration D

### Start
Use an away waste knot, version A or B, using the method described in Chapter 1.

### The Stitch
There are many variations of satin stitch, with geometric satin stitch being the most common version used on samplers. This stitch is easily worked by wrapping the thread over the appropriate number of fabric threads, working from one end of the design area to the other. See Illustrations A and C. This stitch usually requires more than one thread for adequate coverage.

### The Back
The back appears similar to the front, except the stitches have a slight angle. See Illustrations B and D.

### Changing Threads
Run the new threads under the old section of threads and the old threads under the new section of threads. This applies except at the end of a section.

### Ending Threads
Run the thread under the stitches on the back of the fabric. It may be necessary to backstitch around a thread when the stitches are too long to hold the thread securely.

### Turning Corners
Turning corners is not applicable to this stitch.

## Difficulties and Hints

Keeping the threads smooth is difficult, yet this is essential to the finished appearance of the stitch. A laying tool can be purchased and used to keep the threads in place, side by side, while pulling the threads through the fabric. See Illustration E. (A #22 needle or a collar stay can also be used as a laying tool.) Hold the laying tool against the thread, pressing the thread against the fabric. Pull the stitch through the fabric, keeping the threads side by side against the laying tool. This should result in a smooth stitch appearance without twisting of the threads.

Another technique is to use one thread, repeating the stitch twice, or as many times as needed for coverage, in each hole. This technique allows the individual placement of each thread. This is helpful when working with a thick or thin thread in the fabric.

Illustration F shows another advantage to single-thread stitching when satin stitches are placed against a different stitch. In this case, the satin stitch will occasionally roll over, partially covering the adjacent stitch. Using single-thread stitching results in a clean, neat look.

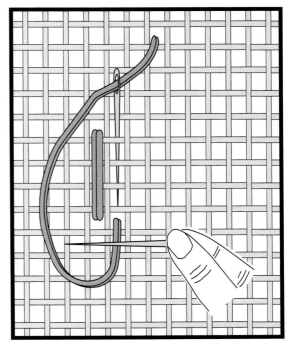

Illustration E

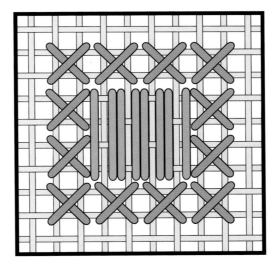

Illustration F

# Kloster-Block Stitch

Kloster block stitch is a geometric satin stitch used in whitework embroidery found in samplers from the sixteenth and seventeenth centuries, as well as Hardanger embroidery. This technique was commonly used with cutwork.

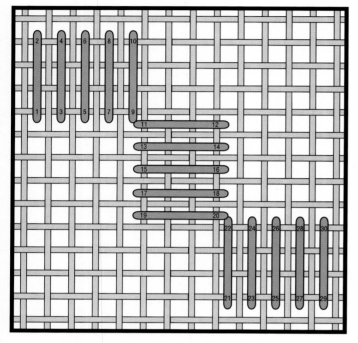

Illustration A

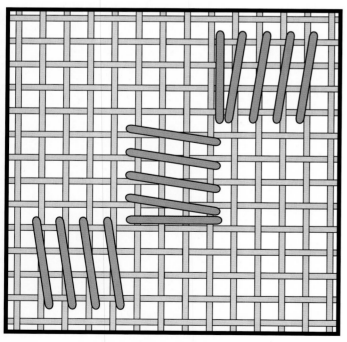

Illustration B

### Start
Use an away waste knot, version A, using the method described in Chapter 1.

### The Stitch
Kloster-block stitch is worked using an odd number of stitches over an even number of threads, with the basic grouping consisting of five threads over four threads of the fabric. When worked on the diagonal, the stitches rotate. See Illustration A.

### The Back
The back appears as diagonal stitches. See Illustration B.

### Changing Threads
Use the method described in Chapter 1.

### Ending Threads
Run the thread under the stitches on the back of the fabric.

### Turning Corners
Follow the step numbering sequence in Illustration A.

### Difficulties and Hints
When rotating the stitch on a diagonal, make sure the thread does not carry across an open area.

# Hungarian Stitch

Hungarian stitch is a smooth-textured stitch. It can be used as a background stitch or in any geometric design where a diamond-shaped stitch can be utilized.

### Start
Use an away waste knot, version A, using the method described in Chapter 1.

### The Stitch
Like Parisian stitch, Hungarian stitch consists of a group of vertical stitches over two threads, over four threads, and then over two threads. See Illustration A. Although the stitch works best in a diagonal stitching pattern, Hungarian stitch can be worked horizontally. See Illustration B.

### The Back
The back of this stitch appears as straight and slanted stitches. See Illustration C.

### Changing Threads
Use the method described in Chapter 1.

### Ending Threads
Run the thread under the stitches on the back of the fabric.

### Turning Corners
Turning corners is not applicable to this stitch.

### Difficulties and Hints
Hungarian stitch is a durable stitch suitable for use in areas where heavy surface wear can be expected, such as footstools and pillows. The extra padding on the back of this stitch gives it long-wearing capabilities, an important feature for items used often.

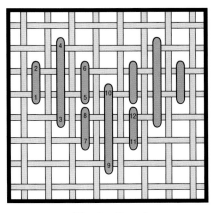

Illustration A

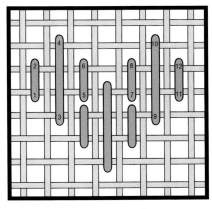

Illustration B

Illustration C

# Parisian Stitch

Parisian stitch, a variation of satin stitch, is worked in a pattern of varying, vertical stitch lengths. This stitch is used as a background or filling stitch.

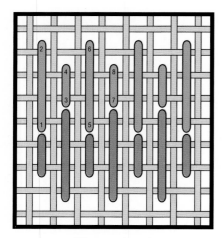

Illustration A

### Start
Use an away waste knot, version A or B, using the method described in Chapter 1.

### The Stitch
Parisian stitch is worked in vertical stitches in a pattern of over four threads, over two threads, over four threads, over two threads. See Illustration A. Parisian stitch creates a very smooth texture and is useful for blending rows of color because of the zigzag pattern created by the stitch.

### The Back
The back appears as diagonal stitches. See Illustration B.

### Changing Threads
Use the method described for satin stitch.

### Ending Threads
Use the method described for satin stitch.

### Turning Corners
Turning corners is not applicable to this stitch.

### Difficulties and Hints
Although Parisian stitch is an easy stitch to work, compensation stitches may be required to provide a completed appearance. This is most noticed when the stitch is placed against a diagonal area.

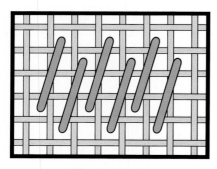

Illustration B

# Irish Stitch (Florentine Stitch, Flame Stitch)

Irish stitch has remained one of the most popular stitches for several centuries. The dramatic effects achieved by working this stitch have been used in upholstery and many other household items. Irish stitch is also called Florentine stitch and flame stitch.

## Start
Use an away waste knot, version A, using the method described in Chapter 1.

## The Stitch
Irish stitch consists of zigzag patterns of staggered, vertical stitches. The basic pattern is worked using vertical stitches over four threads, which are staggered every two threads. See Illustration A. The numbering sequence of the stitches as shown results in the most coverage possible on the back of the fabric. This makes Irish stitch a desirable technique for stitching fabrics that will be used as upholstery. After the first row of stitches is in place, subsequent rows will follow this basic pattern. Making each row a different shade (or color) adds interest and excitement to this stitch.

## The Back
The back appears as long, diagonal stitches, except at the turning points, where a short, diagonal stitch will be seen. See Illustration B.

## Changing Threads
Use the method described in Chapter 1.

## Ending Threads
Run the thread under the stitches on the back of the fabric.

## Turning Corners
Turning corners is not applicable to this stitch.

## Difficulties and Hints
Stitch lengths can be varied, creating infinite possibilities for this stitch.

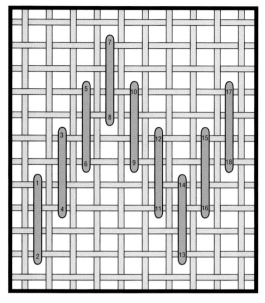

Illustration A

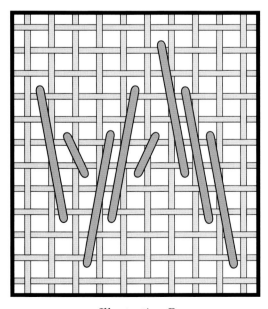

Illustration B

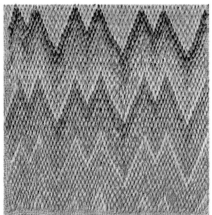

*Reproduction by permission of the Syndics of the Fitzwilliam Museum, Cambridge, England*

77

# Brick Stitch (Long and Short Stitch)

Brick stitch is a smooth-textured satin stitch that is similar to Irish stitch. This stitch is used for shading effects in the blending of colors.

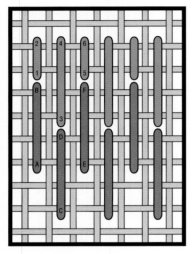

Illustration A

*Start*
Use an away waste knot, version A, using the method described in Chapter 1.

*The Stitch*
The first row of brick stitch is worked using a combination of long and short stitches. Each stitch in the following rows will be of equal length. See Illustration A.

*The Back*
The back appears as diagonal stitches. See Illustration B.

*Changing Threads*
Use the method described in Chapter 1.

*Ending Threads*
Run the thread under the stitches on the back of the fabric.

*Turning Corners*
Turning corners is not applicable to this stitch.

*Difficulties and Hints*
Silk threads, when used to work brick stitch, give a satin finish to the embroidery.

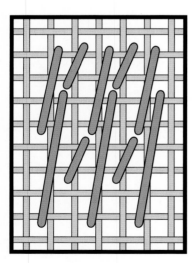

Illustration B

# Gobelin Stitch (Encroaching Gobelin Stitch)

Gobelin stitch was developed to mimic tapestry embroideries. It is often used as a background stitch and works well in the application of shading.

## Start
Use an away waste knot, version A, using the method described in Chapter 1.

## The Stitch
Gobelin stitch consists of diagonal stitches that are two threads in height and one thread wide, worked in a vertical pattern. See Illustration A.

## The Back
The back appears as diagonal stitches. See Illustration B.

## Changing Threads
Use the method described for satin stitch.

## Ending Threads
Use the method described for satin stitch.

## Turning Corners
Turning corners is not applicable to this stitch.

## Difficulties and Hints
A variation of this stitch is the encroaching Gobelin stitch. The encroachment can be worked in varying degrees, over one, two, or three threads, into the previous row of stitching. The degree of encroachment depends on the height of the Gobelin stitch. This stitch is one of the better techniques for shading, due to the varying encroaching depths. See Illustration C for the front of the stitch. See Illustration D for the back of the stitch.

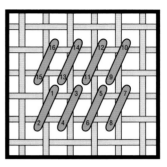

Illustration A

Illustration B

*Reproduction by permission of the Syndics of the Fitzwilliam Museum, Cambridge, England*

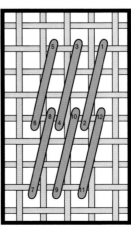

Illustration C

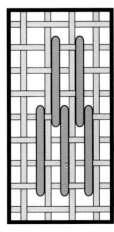

Illustration D

# Tent Stitch (Half Cross Stitch, Basketweave Stitch)

Tent stitch has been used continually since the sixteenth century. Tent stitch and cross stitch are probably the two stitches most frequently used by needleworkers today. This technique has been used for pictorial hangings, upholstery, and clothing. From petit point to coarse canvas, tent stitch is most versatile in its uses.

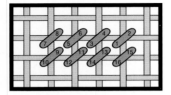

Illustration A

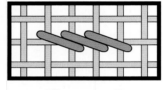

Illustration B

### Start
Use an away waste knot, version A or B, using the method described in Chapter 1.

### The Stitch
Tent stitch consists of diagonal stitches worked over the intersection of canvas or fabric threads. These diagonal stitches may be worked horizontally (see Illustration A) or diagonally (see Illustration C). When worked on the diagonal, this stitch is known as basketweave.

### The Back
The back appears as diagonal stitches over the intersection of two threads. Heavy thread coverage on the back makes tent stitch popular for upholstery uses. See Illustration B.

### Changing Threads
Use the method described in Chapter 1.

### Ending Threads
Run the thread under the stitches on the back of the fabric, using the same, flowing manner used to work the stitch. Do not go against the grain.

### Turning Corners
All stitches should be placed in the same direction unless the pattern dictates otherwise.

### Difficulties and Hints
One of the basic rules of embroidery is to bring the thread up in an empty hole and take the thread down in a filled hole to create a neat appearance. However, with this stitch, that is not possible on every second row of stitching.

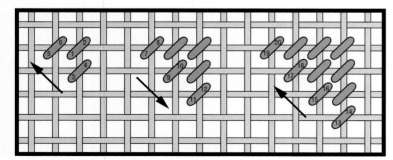

Illustration C

*Chapter Five*

# Straight Stitch Family

The six stitches that make up this chapter are worked using straight stitches, usually following the format of a straight line. The challenging double running stitch is a favorite with stitchers who work sixteenth- and seventeenth-century-style samplers. Made popular by the paintings of Hans Holbein the Younger (1497-1543), court painter for Henry VIII and Jane Seymore, double running stitch, which embellished the opulent garments of the period, became known as Holbein stitch. In a similar manner, the stitch took the name Span-ish stitch after 1501, when Katherine of Aragon came to England and encouraged the use of Spanish-style embroidery, rich in blackwork and encompassing double running stitch. Double running stitch is suited for use on linens, clothing, and other articles that are reversible. Backstitch and running stitch are simple forms of straight stitch; outline stitch and stem stitch are applications of straight stitches used to create curved lines; and faggot stitch is often used to add dimension and texture to whitework areas of samplers.

# Running Stitch

Running stitch is the most simple of all stitches. This stitch can be used to connect fabrics, as a decorative border, or as a filling stitch. This technique is the base stitch of double running stitch.

### Start
Use an away waste knot, version A, using the method described in Chapter 1.

### The Stitch
The stitch weaves in and out of the fabric over a designated number of fabric threads. Illustration A shows the stitch worked over and under two threads.

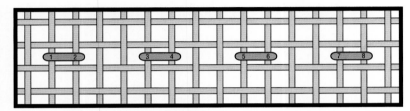

Illustration A

### The Back
The back of this reversible stitch appears the same as the front.

### Changing Threads
Use the method described in Chapter 1.

### Ending Threads
Wrap the thread around stitches on the back of the fabric.

### Turning Corners
There are no special instructions for turning corners as this stitch can be worked to follow any line.

### Difficulties and Hints
Illustration B shows running stitch used as a filling-stitch technique. To work running stitch as a filling stitch, run the thread under the outline (in this case cross stitch), and work running stitch to the other side of the design area. Run the thread under the cross stitches to the next row, rather than across open areas of the fabric. This will eliminate the possibility of a diagonal line being seen from the front.

Illustration B

# Double Running Stitch

Double running stitch has a long history. This stitch has the appearance of a line drawing and is completely reversible. The same design should be seen on the front and back. See photos on pages 40 and 87.

### Start

Use an away waste knot, version A, using the method described in Chapter 1.

### The Stitch

The stitch is worked in two journeys. The first journey places a running stitch that follows the design line. On the return journey, empty spaces of the running stitch are filled. When working a straight line, angle the stitches of the return journey slightly to create a more pleasing effect. See Illustration A. Return stitches will be worked in occupied holes and will not fit end to end with stitches worked on the first journey. The return-journey stitch must either be placed below or above the existing stitch. To create the illusion of a straight line, place one end of the return-journey stitch above the existing stitch and the other below the existing stitch. See Illustration B. Follow a consistent placement pattern for uniformity of appearance.

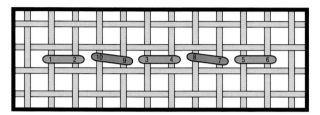

Illustration A

Illustration B

Illustration C details an area branching off the main route of the design. Work the side area all the way to the end and retrace the design to return to the point where the branch began. Sometimes the side trips have side trips. See Illustration D. Side trips must be completed before moving on to another section; otherwise a route will not exist to get back to the main route. These side trips and designs can become very intricate; remember to always complete each section completely as it is reached.

### The Back

The back of this reversible stitch appears the same as the front.

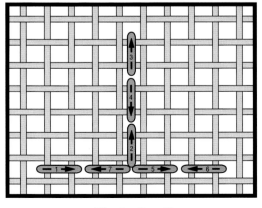

Illustration C

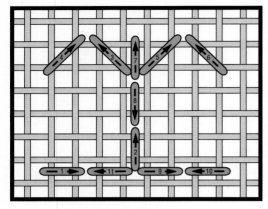

Illustration D

### Changing Threads

Bring the thread to the front and leave it hanging out of the way of the stitching. See Illustration E. Start the new thread with an away waste knot, coming up in the same opening where the old thread was brought to the front of the fabric. Repeat the sequence to complete the design area.

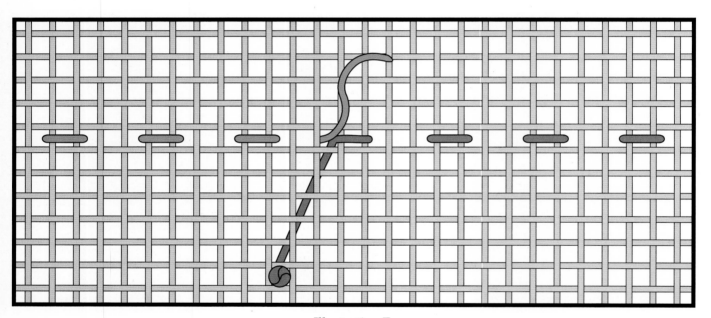

Illustration E

### Ending Threads

End threads only into solidly worked areas. Work the ending threads into areas where both journeys have been completed. Illustrations F and G show this technique. Bring the old thread over one thread of the fabric to the back. Using a sharp needle, penetrate the design (stitching) threads and fabric threads, carrying the needle in the same direction as the stitching and hiding the thread inside the fabric and design (stitching) threads. See Illustration I. Illustration H shows a cutaway section of the fabric and the piercing of threads by the needle.

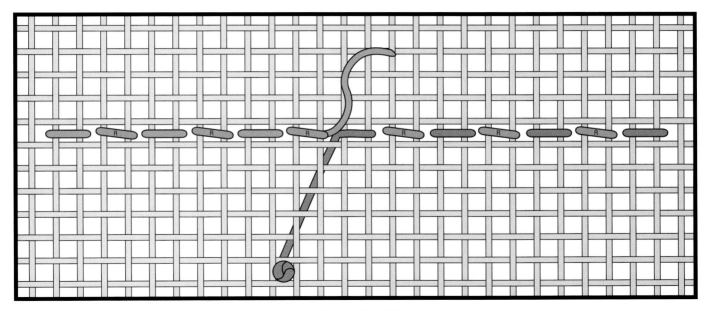

Illustration F

Illustration G shows the stitch that loops over one thread and goes to the back of the fabric. End the thread to the right; end the new thread to the left. This technique allows the threads to cross over one another and eliminates the ending of two threads in the same area or same direction.

Illustrations J and K show the ending of an away waste knot. When ending an away waste knot, the return thread should stop three or four stitches from the location of the away waste knot. See Illustration J. Thread the needle with the away-waste-knot thread and fill in any remaining stitches back to the return thread. End the thread as shown in Illustrations K and L.

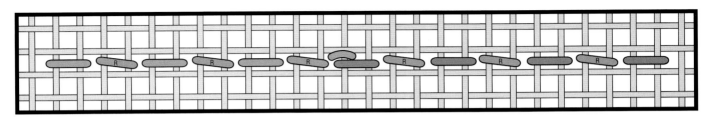

Illustration G

Illustration H

## Turning Corners
The stitch can be turned as needed.

## Difficulties and Hints
When using an away waste knot in double running stitch, allow three inches for the away-waste-knot thread. It is preferable to allow extra thread that may be needed to fill in stitches at the end of the design. As tapestry needles do not easily penetrate fabric threads, use a sharp needle, such as a #9 quilting needle, to end the away-waste-knot or end threads. Plotting the design direction or mapping the direction of travel is best accomplished prior to stitching. This gives a plan for accomplishing the return journey.

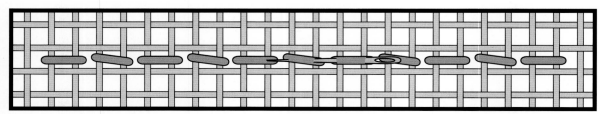

Illustration I

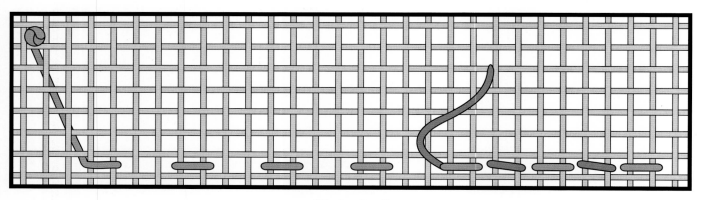

Illustration J

*Reproduction by permission of the Syndics of the Fitzwilliam Museum, Cambridge, England*

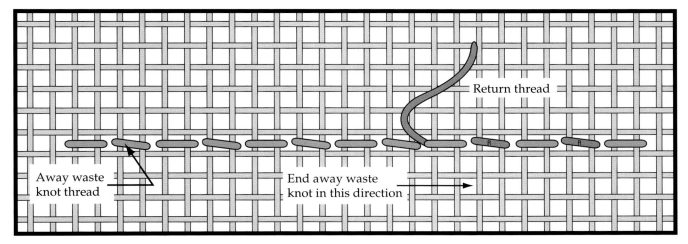

Return thread

Away waste
knot thread

End away waste
knot in this direction

Illustration K

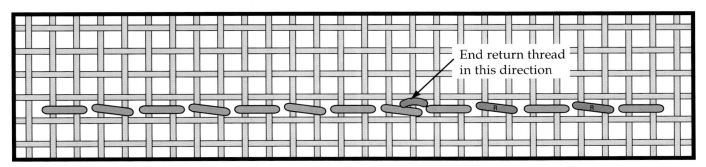

End return thread
in this direction

Illustration L

*Reproduction by permission of the Syndics of the*
*Fitzwilliam Museum, Cambridge, England*

# Outline Stitch, Stem Stitch

Outline stitch and stem stitch can be used to work curved or straight lines of stitches. Outline stitch and stem stitch create a slim line of stitching that can be easily curved. These stitches can be used to work vines, limbs of trees, veins in leaves, and to outline any design.

Illustration A

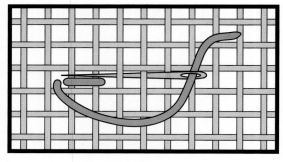

Illustration B

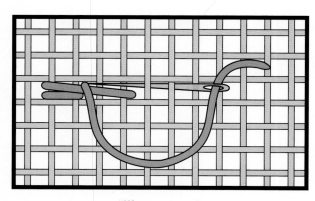

Illlustration C

### Start
Use an away waste knot, version A, using the method described in Chapter 1.

### The Stitch
The thread is held below the row of stitching to work outline stitch. Stem stitch is worked in the same manner, with the thread held above the row of stitching. Illustrations A, B, C, and D show the outline stitch. Illustrations E, F, and G show the stem stitch. These stitches are worked by gathering two threads of the fabric on the needle. The thread is then carried across four threads to the right. Repeat the sequence to continue across the design area. This technique results in a slightly slanted stitch with a very smooth finish.

### The Back
The backs of these reversible stitches appear as lines of backstitch. See Illustration H.

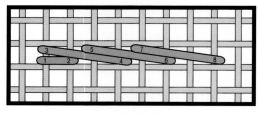

Illustration D

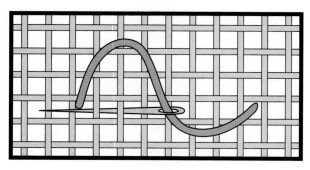

Illustration E

### Changing Threads
Use the method described in Chapter 1.

### Ending Threads
Run the thread under the stitches on the back of the fabric and wrap the thread around the stitches.

### Turning Corners
These stitches can be curved very neatly; however, when turning corners or curves, make sure the stitches do not slant inward toward the inside of the corner or curve. Shorter stitches may be needed to create the corners and curves.

### Difficulties and Hints
In some applications, combinations of these two stitches work well together. For instance, this technique may be used in constructing the bark of a tree. This is accomplished by taking one stitch with the thread going below the line of stitching and the next stitch is placed with the thread going above the line of stitching. Alternate the stitches in this manner completely across the line of stitching. This creates a very unique appearance for tree bark. See Illustrations I, J, and K.

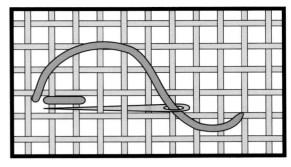

Illustration F

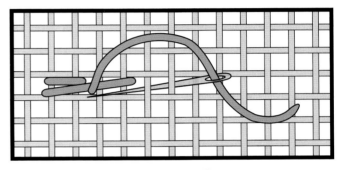

Illustration G

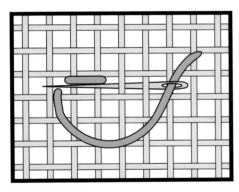

Illustration J

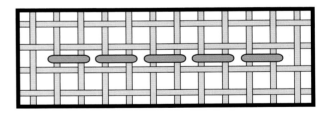

Illustration H

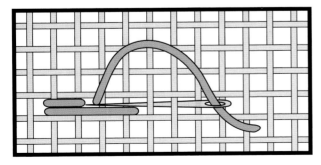

Illustration K

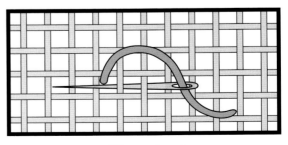

Illustration I

89

# Backstitch

Backstitch is an elementary stitch technique. This technique is used as an outline, a border, or as a straight row of stitching.

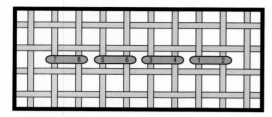

Illustration A

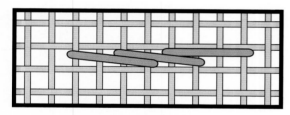

Illustration B

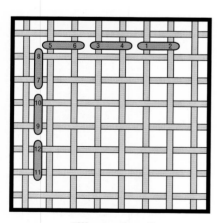

Illlustration C

### Start
Use an away waste knot, version A, using the method described in Chapter 1.

### The Stitch
Bring the thread to the front of the fabric. Count two threads to the right and carry the thread to the back of the fabric. Count four threads to the left and carry the thread to the front of the fabric. Count two threads to the right and carry the thread to the back of the fabric. Repeat the sequence to complete the design. See Illustration A.

### The Back
The back appears the same as the front of outline stitch. See Illustration B.

### Changing Threads
Use the method described in Chapter 1.

### Ending Threads
Wrap the thread around the stitches on the back of the fabric.

### Turning Corners
See Illustration C for the numbering sequence used for turning corners.

### Difficulties and Hints
When turning corners, a diagonal stitch is placed in the corner on the fabric back. If worked on a loosely woven fabric, the diagonal stitch may be seen.

## Faggot Stitch

Faggot stitch has an open and lacy look and is used in pulled thread and whitework applications. This stitch is found in many samplers of the seventeenth century and in many whitework embroideries. Faggot stitch has a distinct texture. Pulling the stitch results in patterns that tend to create shadows required in whitework embroideries. Faggot stitch works well with threads and fabrics that are similar in color.

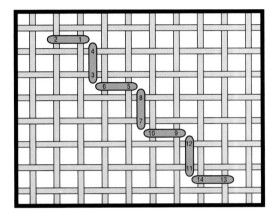

Illustration A

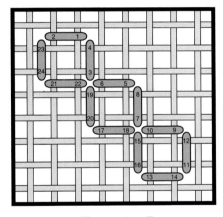

Illustration B

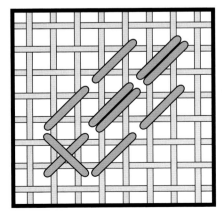

Illustration C

### Start
Use an away waste knot, version A, using the method described in Chapter 1.

### The Stitch
Faggot stitch is a simple backstitch worked in a stair-step motion. See Illustration A. Note that the stitch goes into the back of the previous stitch and the needle travels diagonally down to the next stitch. Two journeys are required to complete the stitch. See Illustration B.

### The Back
The back of this reversible stitch appears as three rows of diagonal stitches, with the center line having a double row of stitches. See Illustration C.

### Changing Threads
Use the method described in Chapter 1.

### Ending Threads
Run the thread under the stitches on the back of the fabric. Be careful not to carry the thread across any open holes created by the stitch.

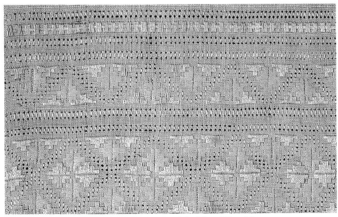

*Reproduction by permission of the Syndics of the Fitzwilliam Museum, Cambridge, England*

91

## Turning Corners

A cross stitch is formed on the back of the fabric when a corner is worked on the fabric front. Illustrations B and D show turning corners. Illustrations C and E show the back of these turns.

## Difficulties and Hints

Ending the thread is probably the most difficult aspect of this stitch. Keep tension consistent throughout the stitching of faggot stitch.

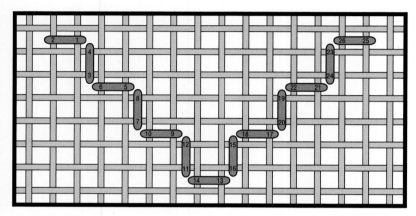

Illustration D

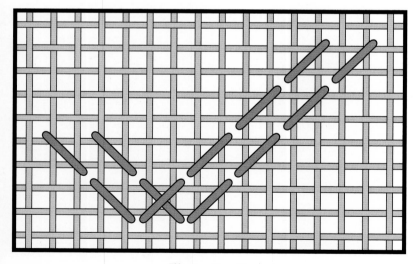

Illustration E

92

# Chapter Six

# *Drawn Thread Techniques*

The techniques and stitches described in this chapter were used as early as the 1500s to create the portion of samplers known as whitework. This monochromatic work, which resembled lace, was achieved using a combination of cutwork and drawn-thread sections and was usually outlined or set apart with hemstitch. Whitework created by using drawn-thread techniques was popular in the sixteenth and seventeenth centuries and was incorporated in samplers to record the patterns used in the garments and household items of that period. Because color is not an element of design in the whitework areas of a sampler, texture becomes the primary focus. The beauty and dimensional depth of whitework is achieved through the shadowing effect created by detached stitches and drawn-thread sections. Drawn-thread work has historically been created using linen thread on a linen ground; however, pearl cotton (coton perlé) is often used on a linen cloth in today's stitchery. Drawn-thread work, as the name implies, is worked in an area where thread is withdrawn from the fabric.

# Drawn-Thread Work

Drawn-thread work was found in samplers from the sixteenth and seventeenth centuries. In a time when only nobility was allowed to wear lace, drawn-thread work gave other society classes the opportunity to have the look of lace. Drawn-thread work is stitched tone-on-tone color; however, in these illustrations, color is used for clarity.

## Start

Work four-sided stitch or double hemstitch around the perimeter of the drawn-thread section. For clarity of other illustrations, this stitch is shown only in Illustrations F and G. **Turn the fabric to the back** and outline the area to be worked by stitching a guideline over and under two threads to complete all four sides of the drawn-thread area. See stitches shown in blue in Illustration A. It is important to work a small tacking stitch so that the corners of the guidelines can touch. Place a cutting guide in the center of the drawn-thread area, top to bottom and side to side. Work over and under two threads. See stitches shown in red in Illustration A. Make sure that the guideline threads weave over and under the same threads as in the perimeter.

## The Stitch

After the perimeter guidelines are in place, working on the back of the fabric, cut the two threads beside each red stitch along the cutting guideline. See Illustration A. The scissors symbols show where to cut. In the example shown, there are seven vertical cuts and seven horizon-

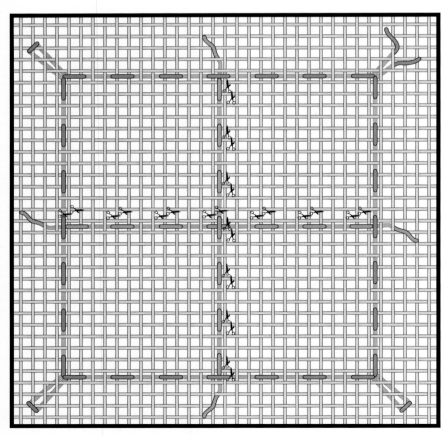

Illustration A

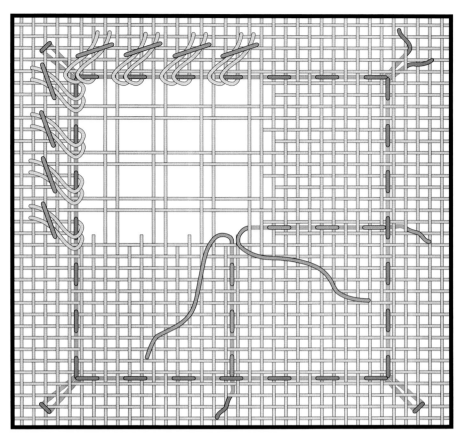

Illustration B

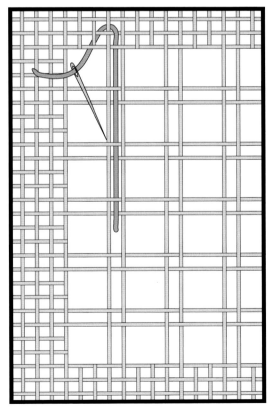

Illustration C

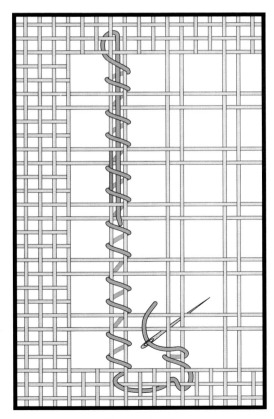

Illustration D

# Dove's-Eye Stitch

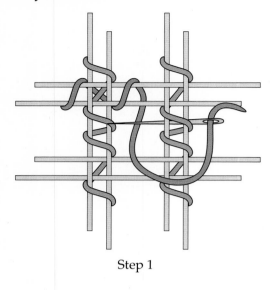

Step 1

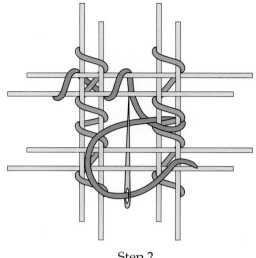

Step 2

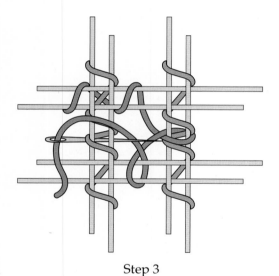

Step 3

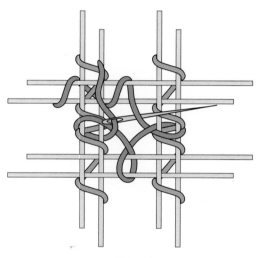

Step 4

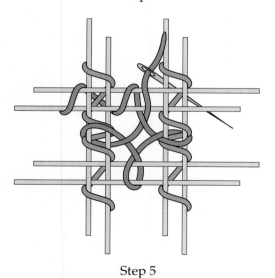

Step 5

Illustration E

tal cuts. With all cutting complete, begin withdrawing the cut threads back to the edge of the perimeter guideline. See Illustration B. Do not take the withdrawn threads past the perimeter guideline. Tack all threads down as they are pulled back on all four sides of the design area to keep them out of the way. Up to this point all work has been done on the back of the fabric. **Turn the fabric to the front.** The remaining threads (or bars) are ready to be overcast. Working vertically and starting at the top-left corner of the design area, begin weaving the thread into the first vertical bar to anchor. See Illustration C. The anchoring thread should begin three to four bar intersections down. In the weave just above the vertical bar, make a tacking stitch to further anchor the thread and to position the thread to begin overcasting the bars. Starting to the left of the bar, wrap the thread around the bar twice in each opening. See Illustration D. Continue in this man-

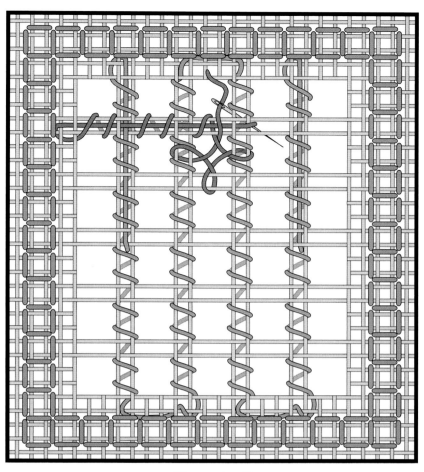

Illustration F

ner to the bottom of the bar, taking a tacking stitch similar to that taken at the top. Carry the thread to the next parallel bar. Turn the fabric 180° to continue working vertically. Repeat the overcast sequence and continue until all bars are overcast. If there is not enough thread to finish the next bar, end the thread into the back of the bar currently being worked. After taking the tacking stitch, weave the thread into the back of the bar under the wrapping threads. Repeat the sequence to start the new bar. Horizontal bars are started and worked in the same manner. However, each bar is ended without carrying the thread over to the next bar. Horizontal bars are worked from left to right. The design for the area is inserted as each horizontal bar is overcast by placing a dove's-eye stitch in the appropriate area. See Illustrations E and F. After all horizontal bars are completed (with a dove's-eye stitch placed in appropriate areas), a satin stitch over two threads is worked around the perimeter between the cutwork area and the four-sided stitch/double hemstitch. See Illustration G.  Remove all guideline threads before working the satin stitch. After completion of the satin stitch, turn the fabric to the back and clip all the drawn threads close to the satin stitch. The area is now finished. An additional weaving stitch may be placed in areas requiring a more solid appearance. See Illustration G.

***The Back***
The back appears very similar to the front.

***Changing Threads***
See "The Stitch."

***Ending Threads***
See "The Stitch."

***Turning Corners***
Turning corners is not applicable to this technique.

***Difficulties and Hints***
Buttonhole stitch may be worked in place of the satin stitch and four-sided stitch. A practice piece is recommended for becoming familiar with the techniques before cutting on the actual piece of embroidery.

Illustration G

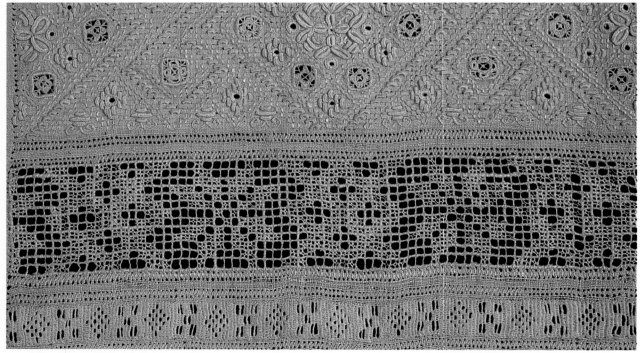

# Double Hemstitch

Double hemstitch is used to work a perimeter around drawn-thread work. This stitch is also used as a decorative technique between rows of drawn threads. See photo on page 98.

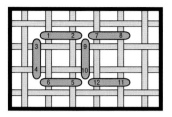

Illustration A

### Start
Use an away waste knot, version A, using the method described in Chapter 1.

### The Stitch
Double hemstitch appears as a four-sided stitch on the front of the fabric. However, the numbering sequence is quite different. This stitch can be worked as a pulled stitch, creating slight openings in the corners of the stitch. Begin this stitch by working a horizontal stitch 1–2. See Illustration A. Bring the thread back to the front of the fabric at 3, sharing a common hole with 1. Work a vertical stitch 3–4, then a horizontal stitch 5–6. From 6, carry the thread diagonally to 2 to complete the stitch. Repeat the sequence to complete the stitch area.

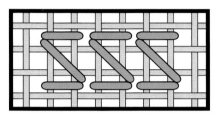

Illustration B

### The Back
The back of the stitch appears as a backward Z. See Illustration B.

### Changing Threads
Use the method described in Chapter 1.

### Ending Threads
Run the thread under the stitches on the back of the fabric.

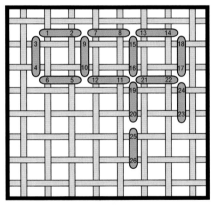

Illustration C

### Turning Corners
See Illustrations C and D for two methods of turning corners. Following these methods will sometimes place the thread sequence in a different order from that shown in Illustration A.

### Difficulties and Hints
Use sturdy thread, such as #12 pearl cotton (coton perlé) or linen thread, when working this stitch with drawn-thread work. These threads will be more durable under the stress that is applied when working pulled stitches.

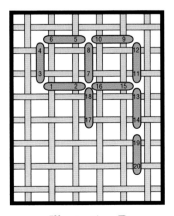

Illustration D

# Hemstitch

1. Working on the back of the fabric, count out three threads from the design area and cut the fourth thread a minimum of four inches from the corners of the design. It is best to cut this thread at the center point of each side. Unweave the cut thread back to the corners and reweave it into the fabric. See Illustration A.

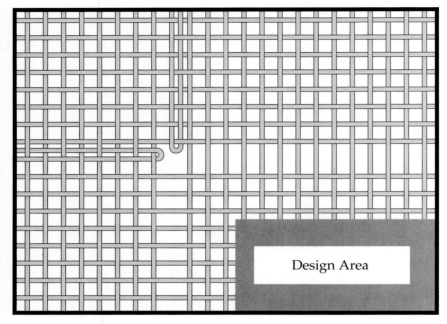

Illustration A

2. After the threads are rewoven in all four corners, score the fabric. See Illustration B for placement of scoring. See Illustration C for the technique of scoring fabric. Count out the appropriate number of threads from the cut-thread line to place score line 1. See Illustration D for a thread-

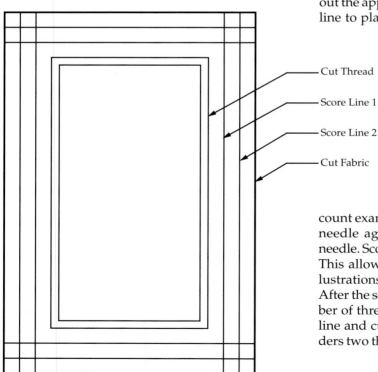

Cut Thread

Score Line 1

Score Line 2

Cut Fabric

count example. Lay the fabric on a hard surface, place the needle against the fabric, and pull the fabric, not the needle. Score the entire length of the fabric on all four sides. This allows a clean fold without pressing. Following Illustrations B and D, score a second line on all four sides. After the second score line is in place, count an equal number of threads, minus two threads, past the second score line and cut the fabric on all four sides. Cutting the borders two threads more narrow will create a smoother fold.

Illustration B

3. Miter the corners. Fold the fabric into the corner. See Illustration E. Cut the excess fabric from the corner and continue to fold. See Illustrations F and G. Fold the sides of the piece in the same manner and pin in place. Baste the hemstitch in place with sewing thread and remove pins. This is important, for pins are difficult to work around when hemstitching.

4. Hemstitch the folded edge in place. See Illustration H. Begin using an away waste knot, version B. Anchor the hemstitch to the fold. See Illustration I. After the thread is secured, cut off the waste knot. When corners are reached, stitch the corners closed on the miter with an invisible stitch up the seam.

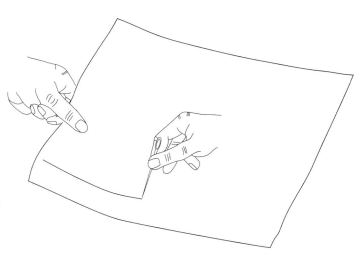

Illustration C

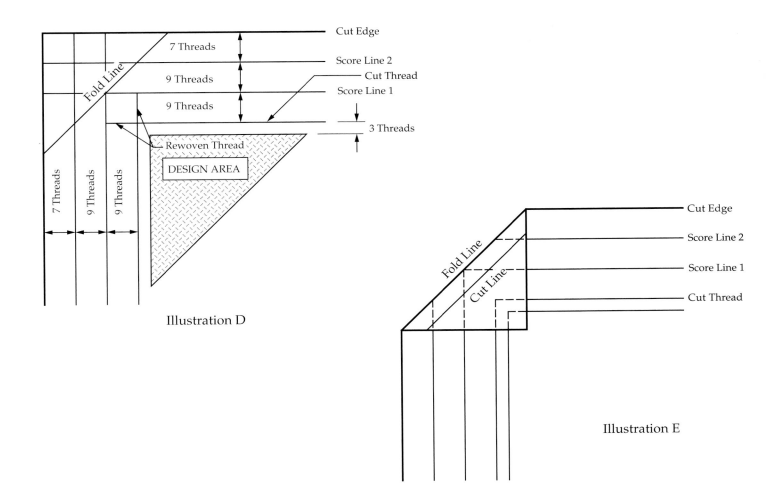

Illustration D

Illustration E

101

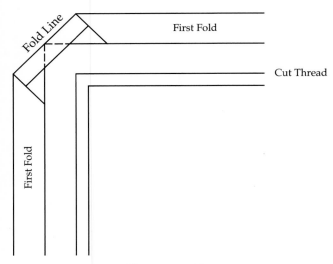

Illustration F

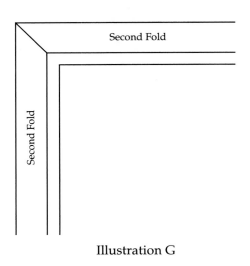

Illustration G

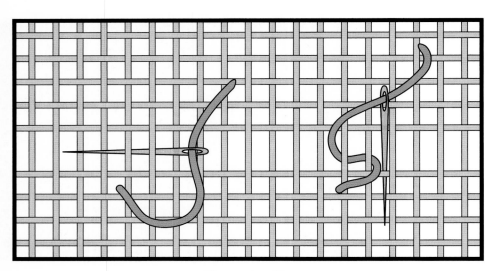

Illustration H

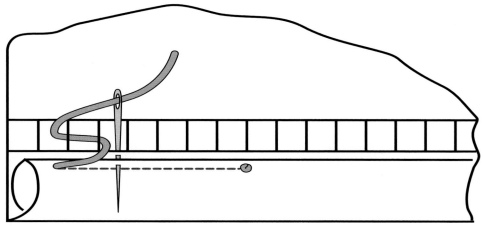

Illustration I

102

*Chapter Seven*

# Looped Stitch Family

The eleven stitches grouped in this chapter are most often used to create wide, impressive borders or to fill large, open areas within a design. All the stitches, with the exception of the lattice stitch, are secured to the ground cloth by using a looped, or tacking, stitch. The base thread of lattice stitch is secured to the fabric with a two-step tacking stitch, in the shape of an X or a cross. Many spot-motif samplers from the sixteenth and seventeenth centuries were heavily embellished with geometric motifs worked using the stitches in this chapter. Ladder stitch and braid stitch were commonly worked in metal threads. The stitches in this grouping are all looped stitches, worked either by looping around themselves or around other stitches.

# Interlacing Stitch

Interlacing stitch is another version of Maltese cross stitch. Interlacing stitch has been found in spot-motif samplers from the seventeenth century. This stitch makes a very intricate and impressive border.

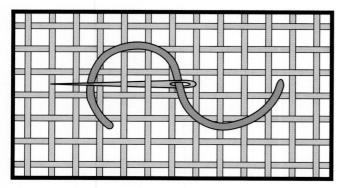

Illustration A

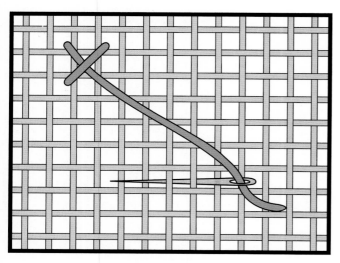

Illustration B

### Start
Use an away waste knot, version A, using the method described in Chapter 1.

### The Stitch
Work herringbone stitch as a base for this stitch. It is important that all herringbone stitches are placed correctly, with stitches going over and under the correct sequence of threads. Illustration A shows the thread held above while the stitch is worked. This allows the correct thread to be placed on top. The bottom stitch is shown in Illustration B. Work to the end of the row and take a stitch in the same manner in the center edge as in Illustration A. Turn the work 180° and work in the same manner. The return journey will require weaving under the existing thread in an upward movement to work the top stitch. This is important to guarantee the weaving will be worked correctly. See Illustrations C and D. Weave the thread around the herringbone stitch along the top edge. See Illustration C. At the end of the top section, weave the thread around the end herringbone stitch and turn the fabric 180° to continue. It will be necessary to weave into the weaving thread on the return journey.

### The Back
The back appears as herringbone stitch, with very few stitches seen on the back of the fabric. The weaving thread will not be seen on the back except where the threads are ended.

### Changing Threads
If it is necessary to change threads in the process of weaving, bring the old thread to the back of the fabric in a location similar to that shown in Illustration D. Bring the new thread up in the same hole and continue stitching in the same manner as before.

### Ending Threads
Wrap the thread around the existing stitches on the back of the fabric.

### Turning Corners
Turning corners is not applicable to this stitch.

## Difficulties and Hints

Ending thread is the most difficult part of this technique due to the lack of threads on the back of the fabric. Be very aware of which threads are worked over and under so that the weaving sequence can be worked properly.

This stitch looks best when one color or weight of thread is used for the herringbone stitch and a contrasting thread is used for the weaving stitch.

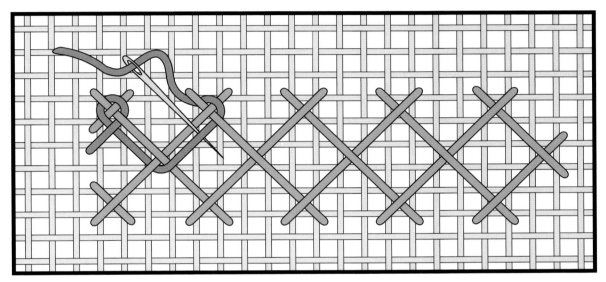

Illlustration C

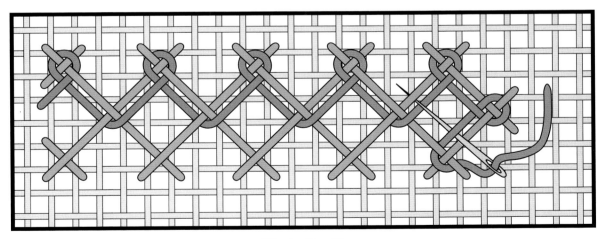

Illustration D

105

# Maltese Cross Stitch

Maltese cross stitch is an intricate, fascinating stitch that appears to loop and weave, with the beginning and ending indeterminable. Maltese cross stitch has been found on spot-motif samplers from the seventeenth century. The stitch can be used to fill backgrounds and to create wide borders.

### Start
Use an away waste knot, version A, using the method described in Chapter 1.

### The Stitch
The background grid must be worked first. See Illustration A. The over-under sequence must be placed perfectly for this weaving stitch to work properly. One grid stitch placed in the wrong position can ruin the intricate weav-

ing pattern. See Illustration B for the weaving sequence. To repeat a sequence, work stitch 19–20 the length of stitch 11–12. This placement will carry the thread down to another section.

### The Back
The back of the stitch shows very few stitches. Most of the thread is placed on the front of the fabric.

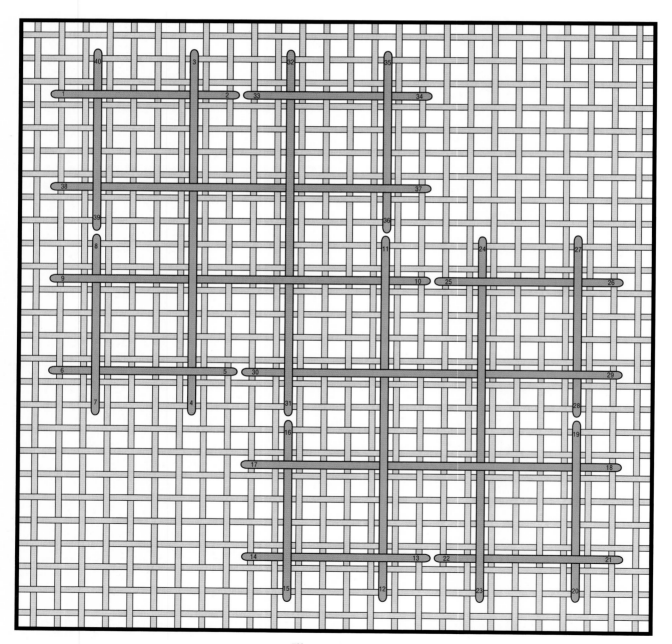

Illustration A

## Changing Threads

The grid threads may be changed at any point where the thread is brought to the back of the fabric. Start with a sufficient length for the weaving thread. Should it become necessary to change the weaving thread, choose a similar area to that of the starting point. A location where the stitch weaves under is best for changing threads.

## Ending Threads

Weave the thread in and out of the stitches on the back of the fabric.

## Turning Corners

Turning corners is not applicable to this stitch in counted-thread uses.

## Difficulties and Hints

Make certain the over-under sequence is in the correct place and that the weaving is placed over and under properly. Create interest in this stitch by using one thread color for the grid thread and another color for the weaving thread.

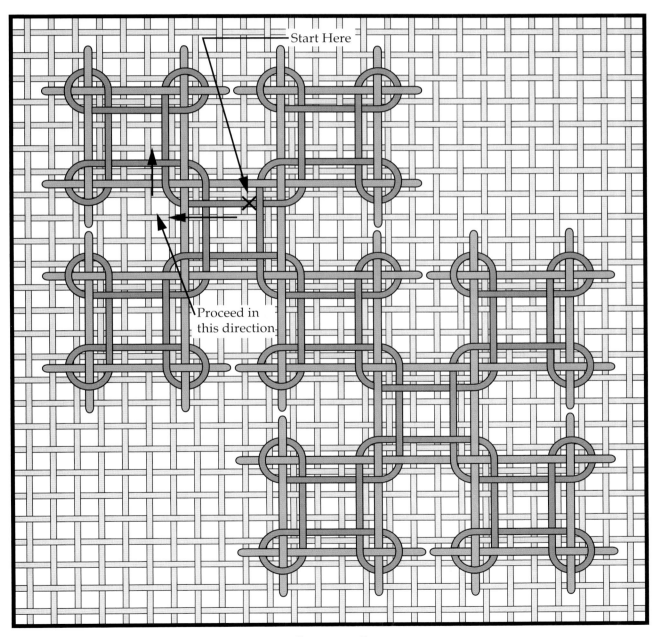

Illustration B

# Chain Stitch, Open Chain Stitch, Cable Chain Stitch

Chain stitch is a basic embroidery stitch. Using this technique creates a neat row of circles that resembles a chain. Chain stitch can be used for borders and works well as a filling stitch. Because of the method used to form the stitch, it adapts to curves easily and can travel in any direction.

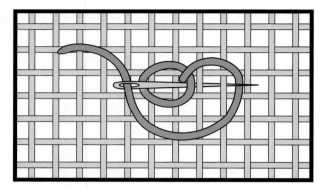

Illustration A

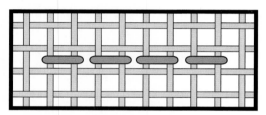

Illustration B

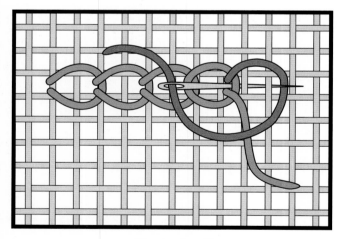

Illustration C

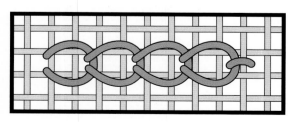

Illustration D

### Start
Use an away waste knot, version A, using the method described in Chapter 1.

### The Stitch (Chain Stitch)
Make a loop with the thread, and hold in place while taking the needle back into the fabric at the point where the thread came to the front. Illustration A shows the stitch worked over two threads. Count two threads to the right and bring the needle through the fabric and over the loop. When the thread is pulled through the fabric, the thread will catch and secure the loop of the first stitch. Work the next stitch in the same manner, with the needle entering the fabric on the inside of the chain stitch just worked. Repeat the sequence for the length of the design area.

### The Back (Chain Stitch)
The back of this reversible stitch appears as backstitch. See Illustration B.

### Changing Threads (Chain Stitch)
Bring the thread to the front as if to start a new stitch, leaving it hanging out of the way of the stitching. See Illustration C. Connect the new thread into the stitches on the back of the fabric, bringing the thread to the front in the same hole as the old thread. Make a loop and work a chain stitch as before. Continue stitching with the new thread. After the new stitches are in place, end the old thread into the back of the new stitches.

### Ending Threads (Chain Stitch)
Bring the thread to the front of the fabric through the loop, as if starting a new stitch. Work a tacking stitch over the next fabric thread, carrying the thread to the back of the fabric. Wrap the thread over the stitches on the back of the fabric. See Illustration D.

### Turning Corners (Chain Stitch)
There are no special instructions for turning corners for the chain stitch. The stitch will flow as required by the design.

### Difficulties and Hints (Chain Stitch)
Use care when removing a misplaced chain stitch. When one stitch is removed, other stitches will pull out easily.

### The Stitch (Open Chain Stitch)

Open chain stitch is worked in much the same manner as chain stitch; however, the thread is not carried to the back of the fabric in the same manner as chain stitch. The needle is held at a slight angle. Begin open chain by bringing the thread to the front of the fabric. Count two threads to the right and angle the needle down two threads to the left. Bring the needle to the front of the fabric, catching the loop of thread. See Illustration E. A second stitch in progress is shown in Illustration F. Illustration H shows several stitches in place.

### The Back (Open Chain Stitch)

The back appears as a row of diagonal stitches. See Illustration G.

### Changing Threads (Open Chain Stitch)

Threads are changed in the same manner as for chain stitch.

### Ending Threads (Open Chain Stitch)

Two tacking stitches are required to end open chain stitch. See Illustration H. End the threads under the slanted stitches on the back of the fabric.

### Turning Corners (Open Chain Stitch)

Turning corners is not applicable to this stitch.

### Difficulties and Hints (Open Chain Stitch)

After making the loop and pulling the needle through the fabric, the loop is left loose until the needle is in the position to start the next stitch. Pull the tension at this point.

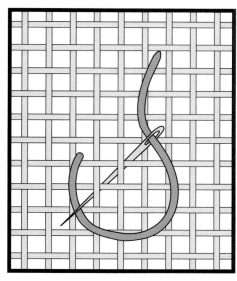

Illustration E

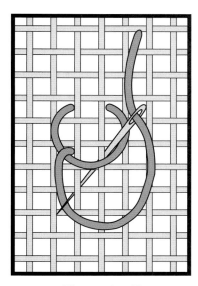

Illustration F

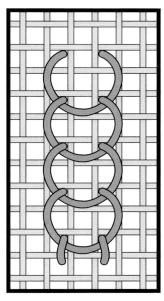

Illustration H

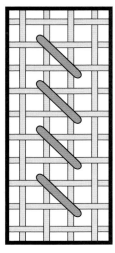

Illustration G

Illustration I

This technique will keep the stitch from being uneven. Metal threads work well for this stitch because they are sturdy and keep their shape.

### The Stitch (Cable Chain Stitch)

Cable chain stitch has the look of a linked chain. To start, twist the thread around the needle. See Illustration I. After the thread is wrapped around the needle, pull the tension on the thread. Place the needle in position to work the next chain stitch. This technique will create a linked effect of a straight stitch between two chain stitches. See Illustration J.

### The Back

The back of this reversible stitch appears as running stitch.

### Changing Threads (Cable Chain Stitch)

Threads are changed in the same manner as for chain stitch.

### Ending Threads (Cable Chain Stitch)

Threads are ended in the same manner as for chain stitch.

### Turning Corners (Cable Chain Stitch)

Turning corners is not applicable to this stitch.

### Difficulties and Hints (Cable Chain Stitch)

Although this stitch appears difficult, with practice this should become an easy technique. Remember to pull the tension on the thread wrapped around the needle before inserting the needle in the fabric to make the chain stitch.

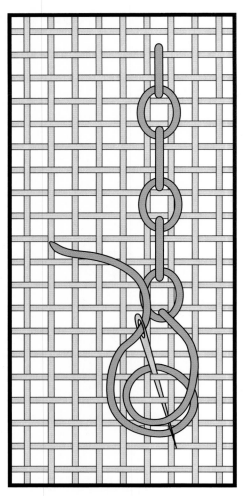

Illustration J

# Ladder Stitch

Ladder stitch is aptly named for its appearance. This stitch, usually worked with metal threads, is found in samplers from the seventeenth century. The stitch has the appearance of horizontal rows with a braided stitch on each side.

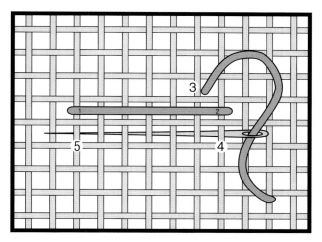

Illustration A

Illustration B

## Start

Use an away waste knot, version A, using the method described in Chapter 1.

## The Stitch

Place a horizontal thread from left to right and bring the needle to the front of the fabric one thread above the stitch and one thread to the left. See Illustration A. Bring the thread down two threads and one thread to the right, aligning the needle with stitch 1–2. Carry the needle under the fabric to the left side. Bring the thread to the front and wrap the thread around the horizontal stitch above. This stitch does not penetrate the fabric but slips easily under the horizontal stitch. See Illustration B. Carry the thread to the right and slip the needle under the diagonal stitch. See Illustration C. This stitch does not penetrate the fabric but slips under the existing stitch on the top of the fabric. Carry the thread down diagonally and enter the fabric below this stitch, penetrating the fabric. Carry the thread across to the left. See Illustration D. Bring the thread to the front of the fabric and wrap the thread around the stitches above. Slip the needle under the looped stitch above. Repeat sequence to complete design.

## The Back

The back appears as horizontal threads, except in the upper-left corner, where a small, diagonal stitch appears. See Illustration E.

111

## Changing Threads

Carry the thread to the back of the fabric on the right, and leave it hanging out of the way of the stitching. Run the new thread under the stitches on the back of the fabric and bring the thread to the front of the fabric on the left. Continue to stitch as before. When the new stitches are in place, carry the old thread under the new stitches on the back of the fabric.

## Ending Threads

Run the thread under the stitches on the back of the fabric. This may be difficult due to the width of the stitches. If the thread does not seem to be adequately anchored, wrap the thread around one of the stitches and continue to carry the thread under the horizontal threads.

## Turning Corners

Turning corners is not applicable to this stitch.

## Difficulties and Hints

In order to be worked properly and result in the correct appearance, this stitch must be worked using a heavy or stiff thread. Threads such as pearl cotton (coton perlé) and metal threads work well for this technique.

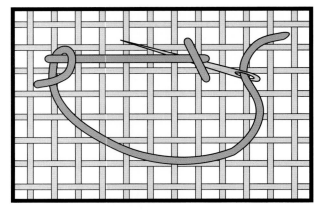

Illustration C

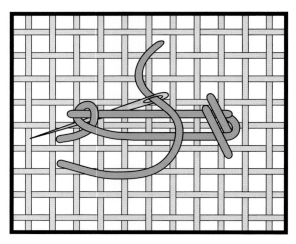

Illustration D

*Reproduction by permission of the Syndics of the Fitzwilliam Museum, Cambridge, England*

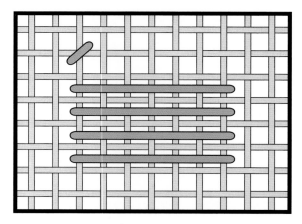

Illustration E

112

# Braid Stitch

Braid stitch was very popular during the seventeenth century. The heavy, ornate nature of the stitch worked well with the styles of the day. The sturdy nature and shape-holding abilities of metal thread make it a good choice for working this stitch.

### Start
Use an away waste knot, version A, using the method described in Chapter 1.

### The Stitch
Bring the thread to the front of the fabric and make a loop with the thread. Pass the needle under the loop to place the threads in the correct position for completing the stitch. Carry the needle under the correct number of threads to create the width of braid desired. See Illustration A. The braid stitch is shown worked over three threads. After passing the needle through the loop and out of the fabric under the three threads, pull the tension. Hook the loop of the thread under the end of the needle and pull the thread through. This creates the braided effect. See Illustration B.

### The Back
The back appears as vertical stitches.

### Changing Threads
Bring the thread to the front of the fabric, and leave it hanging out of the way of the stitching. Run the new thread under the existing stitches on the back and bring the thread to the front of the fabric, using the same hole as for the old thread. This is similar to the methods used for chain stitch. Continue to work the section with the new thread.

### Ending Threads
Take any threads on the fabric front to the back of the fabric. Work thread ends under existing stitches. As stitches on the back of the fabric may be somewhat loose, it may be necessary to wrap the threads around the stitches to adequately secure them.

### Turning Corners
Braid stitch can curve naturally but does not work well in turning sharp corners. If a sharp corner is needed, work the thread to the end of the design area and start a new section of stitching in the proper direction.

### Difficulties and Hints
Insert the needle as shown in Illustration A. Pull the tension, leaving the needle in the fabric. Pull the needle through, adjusting the final tension.

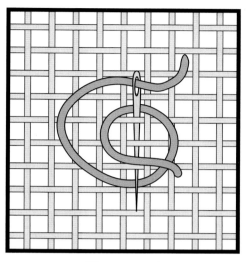

Illustration A

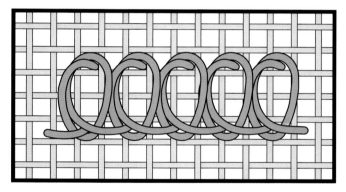

Illustration B

*Reproduction by permission of the Syndics of the Fitzwilliam Museum, Cambridge, England*

# Couching Stitch

Couching stitch is the application of threads to the fabric surface that are too thick to pass through the fabric. This technique can be found in embroideries as early as the first century B.C. Couching is utilized as a decorative filling or border.

### Start
Use an away waste knot, version A, using the method described in Chapter 1 to secure the tacking thread.

### The Stitch
Place the thread to be couched on top of the fabric, leaving a one-to-two-inch tail of thread on each end. Bring the tacking thread to the front of the fabric and work a tacking stitch over the couching thread. Carry the thread to the back of the fabric. Continue to place evenly spaced tacking stitches along the couching thread to secure the length of the thread. See Illustration A.

### The Back
The tacking stitch will be visible on the back of the fabric. See Illustration B.

### Changing Threads
Do not change threads in the middle of a row of stitching. Use an adequate length of thread to complete the design area.

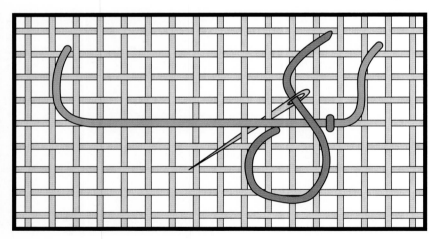

Illustration A

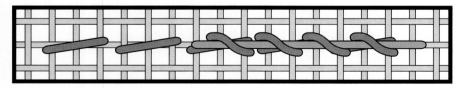

Illlustration B

### Ending Threads
Bring the couching thread to the back of the fabric and lay it atop the tacking threads. See Illustration C. Cut off the tacking thread away waste knot and rethread the needle. Anchor the couching thread by whipstitching with the tacking thread. See Illustration B.

### Turning Corners
The couching stitch can be adapted to any shape.

### Difficulties and Hints
Start this stitch with adequate lengths of thread. Choose an inconspicuous thread as the tacking stitch, unless the tacking thread is to be used as part of the design. For example, when couching gold, metal threads, use a light-yellow thread as the tacking thread. Do not allow the couched thread to loop or wrinkle.

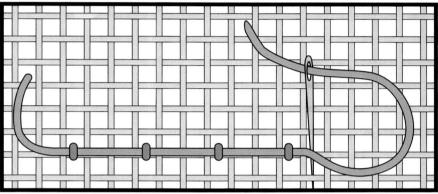

Illustration C

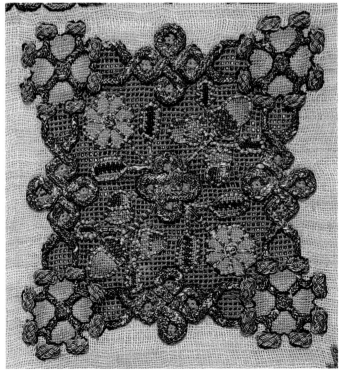

# Queen Stitch (Rococo Stitch)

Queen stitch, also known as rococo stitch, though time-consuming, is one of the loveliest stitches found on works from the seventeenth century. When queen stitch is pulled, a lacy effect is achieved, creating a stitch "fit for a queen." The resulting pattern of the queen stitch is a diamond shape with center tacking stitches.

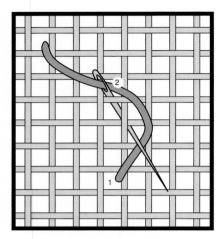

Illustration A

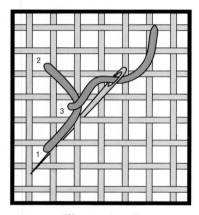

Illustration B

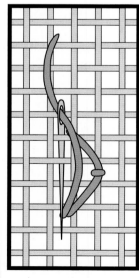

Illustration C

### Start

Use an away waste knot, version A, using the method described in Chapter 1.

### The Stitch

The stitch is composed of four loops of thread that share a common hole at the top and bottom. Each loop is tacked down in the center over a separate thread of fabric. Bring the thread to the front of the fabric at the bottom of the stitch and hold the thread to the right. Count up four threads and carry the thread to the back of the fabric to complete stitch 1–2. See Illustration A. Count two threads down and one thread to the right and bring the thread to the front of the fabric at 3. Pull the thread slightly to create the holes at the top and bottom of the stitch. Place a small, tacking stitch over the vertical thread two threads to the right of the stitch center. See Illustration B. Repeat the sequence for the second vertical stitch. See Illustration C. Illustration D shows the completion of the tacking stitch. Note that the tacking stitch shares a common hole with the previously placed tacking stitch. Repeat the sequence to place the third vertical stitch. See Illustration E. Before pulling the tension on the third vertical stitch, place the loop of thread to the left and insert the needle into the fabric, as seen in Illustration F. This needle placement is necessary for holding the vertical thread in place while pulling the tension. Illustration F shows how tension is pulled on the thread before pulling the needle through the fabric. Repeat the sequence to complete the fourth and final vertical stitch. See Illustration G. Come up at the bottom of the stitch, hold the loop of thread to the right, and complete the stitch. See Illustration H. Remember to hold the loop to the left and insert the needle as shown before pulling the tension. Illustration J shows a single, completed queen stitch. Illustration I shows four completed queen stitches placed together. The points of the diamonds share common holes.

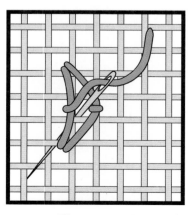

Illustration D

116

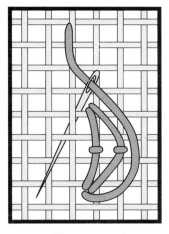

Illlustration E

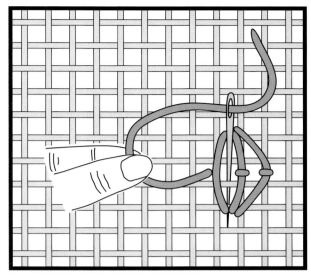

Illustration F

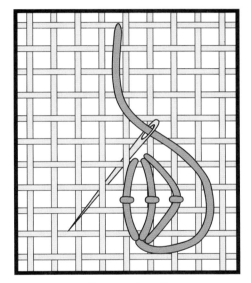

Illustration G

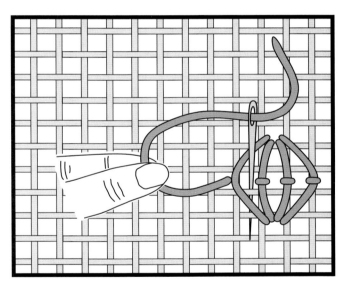

Illustration H

Illustration I

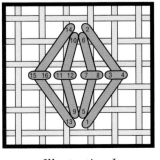

Illustration J

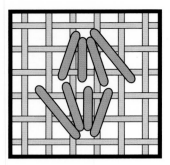

Illustration K

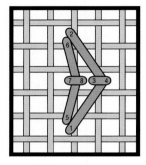

Illustration L

Illustration M

### The Back
The back appears as vertical and diagonal stitches. See Illustration K.

### Changing Threads
Use the method described in Chapter 1.

### Ending Threads
Run the thread under the stitches on the back of the fabric.

### Turning Corners
There are no special techniques for turning corners. The stitch may be worked on its side to create a different texture effect.

### Difficulties and Hints
The most difficult aspect of constructing queen stitch is being able to judge the correct tension on the vertical threads that create the top and bottom holes of the stitch. One of the most common mistakes is simply not pulling these stitches tightly enough. This stitch, when properly constructed, should not appear loose, but rather should appear full and tight with an appearance of a diamond shape on the ground fabric. Queen stitch works well diagonally. Half queen stitches may be used vertically or horizontally to create a straight-line effect in a design. See Illustration L. Illustration M shows four complete queen stitches, two placed horizontally and two placed vertically. The resulting motif was common to samplers from the seventeenth century.

*Reproduction by permission of the Syndics of the Fitzwilliam Museum, Cambridge, England*

# Roman Stitch

Roman stitch is composed of a straight stitch secured by a small, horizontal tacking stitch in its center. This stitch was popular during the seventeenth century and was used in the motif-style sampler. The stitch can be used as a filling stitch to cover areas of the ground fabric.

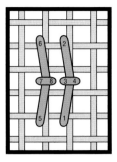

Illustration A

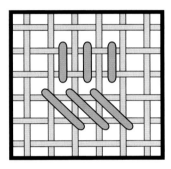

Illustration B

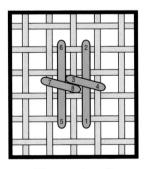

Illustration C

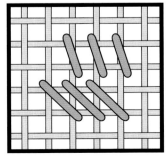

Illustration D

### Start
Use an away waste knot, version A, using the method described in Chapter 1.

### The Stitch
Bring the thread to the front of the fabric at the bottom of the stitch, count four threads up, and carry the thread to the back of the fabric, completing stitch 1–2. See Illustration A. Tacking stitch 3–4 is placed at the mid-point of the stitch, pulling the thread to the right. This creates a slight angle of the vertical straight stitch. Repeat the sequence to complete the design area. Another version of this stitch is shown in Illustration C. Note the placement of the horizontal tacking stitch. The tacking stitch is worked over two threads and the vertical stitch remains straight, giving a more vertical appearance to Roman stitch.

### The Back
The back of version 1 appears as vertical and diagonal stitches. See Illustration B. The back of version 2 appears as diagonal stitches. See Illustration D.

### Changing Threads
Use the method described in Chapter 1.

### Ending Threads
Run the thread under the stitches on the back of the fabric.

### Turning Corners
Use the method described for satin stitch.

### Difficulties and Hints
Roman stitch can be used to fill in leaves, petals of flowers, or any area requiring a satin-stitch appearance. This technique works well over areas requiring long, vertical or horizontal threads of satin stitch. The diagonal tacking stitch adds strength and stability to the placed threads. Use this technique when satin stitch would appear too loose.

*Reproduction by permission of the Syndics of the Fitzwilliam Museum, Cambridge, England*

# Lattice Stitch

Lattice stitch is found in crewelwork as well as in counted-thread work. This stitch can be used to fill large, open areas. This stitch is found in samplers from the seventeenth century but was even more popular during later periods.

Illustration A

Illustration B

### Start

Use an away waste knot, version A, using the method described in Chapter 1.

### The Stitch

This stitch is composed of two parts, the base grid and the tacking stitches. The base grid is worked first and generally is composed of long vertical, horizontal, or diagonal stitches. To keep these stitches stable, a decorative tacking stitch is applied at the intersections of the vertical and horizontal stitches. See Illustrations A and B.

### The Back

Very little thread is placed on the back of the fabric.

### Changing Threads

Threads cannot be changed. End threads under stitches on the back of the fabric and begin a new thread.

### Ending Threads

Run the thread under the stitches on the back of the fabric.

### Turning Corners

Turning corners is not applicable to this stitch.

### Difficulties and Hints

The base grid may be worked using a different thread type or color from the tacking thread. The tacking thread, when worked in a small area, may be a vertical or a horizontal stitch, rather than a combination of both. This stitch can be used to fill any shape since the vertical, horizontal, or diagonal base grid threads may be placed in varying lengths to fit the application.

# The Proper Stitch Sampler

Worked using metallic, silk, and cotton threads, *The Proper Stitch Sampler* incorporates more than 35 stitches, all found in the preceding chapters of this book. The model pictured contains a spot-motif area, a colored-band area, and a whitework area. All motifs and designs are authentic to seventeenth-century English band samplers. Page references in the instructions refer to photos detailing sections of this sampler.

Work the design from the top, starting in the upper-left corner of the fabric. Work motifs, dividing bands, and rows in the order listed in the instructions. Use one strand of thread in the needle, unless otherwise noted. Refer to color code if color is not designated in instructions.

Row 1: Work the 13 motifs following the instructions for each. See photo on page 7.

Motif 1: Work Maltese cross stitch using yellow for the base grid and medium blue for the needleweaving. See Maltese cross stitch, page 106, Illustrations A and B.

Motif 2: Work queen stitch. Note the vertical half-queen stitches on the sides of the strawberries and in the green cap. *pg· 116, 118*

Motif 3: Work Hungarian stitch. *pg·75*

Motif 4: Work the acorn cap in tent stitch, using brown and medium blue. Work the acorn in satin stitch, using yellow. Work couching around the satin stitch, using two strands of gold. See Illustration 1 for details on working acorn cap. *pg· 80, 72+73, 114+115*

Motif 5: Work the diamond shapes of this motif in queen stitch. Work remainder of this motif in chain stitch. *pg·116, 118   pg·108*

Motif 6: Work motif in these stitches: cross, backstitch, and queen. See Illustration 2 for details.

Motif 7: Work the squares of this motif in Algerian eye stitch. Work interlacing stitch between the two rows of Algerian eye stitch, using gold thread. *pg· 68   pg· 104*

Motif 8: Work Irish stitch. Working from the bottom, stitch in the following color order: light rose, medium rose, dark rose, yellow, medium green, and dark green. *pg· 77*

Motif 9: Work diagonal rice stitch. *pg· 28*

Motif 10: Work Roman stitch in areas coded for green thread. Work braid stitch in areas coded for metallic gold thread. See chart for color location. *pg· 119 + pg· 113*

Motif 11: Work ladder stitch using metallic gold. *pg· 111, 112*

Motif 12: Work cable chain stitch using metallic gold. *pg· 110*

Motif 13: Work open chain stitch using metallic gold. *pg· 109*

DB 1, 2: Work reversible cross stitch. Choose the version you prefer. *pg· 13+14 + 118*

Row 2: Work double running stitch using dark blue. See Illustration 3. See photo on page 11. *pg· 83, 86+87*

Row 3: Work the alphabet in cross stitch. Work the numbers in four-sided stitch.

DB 3, 4: Work double-backstitch variation. *pg· 36*

Row 4: Work the base design in double running stitch. See Illustration 4. Work numbered stitches using brown and lettered stitches using dark blue. Work satin stitches in the top portion of the numbered flower, using light rose. Work the base of the flower in satin stitch, using medium green. Work satin stitches in the lettered flower, using medium blue.

Row 5: Work the vine in Montenegrin stitch and diagonal Montenegrin stitch. Work the center of the vine, point A, and the center of the stem in double backstitch and diagonal double backstitch. Work the tendrils attached to the vine in double running stitch, using dark green. Work the veins of the leaves in double running stitch, using brown. Work the outline of the large leaves in diagonal cross stitch and reversible cross stitch. Work the tendrils attached to the grapes in double running stitch, using dark blue. Work the outline of each grape in reversible cross stitch and diagonal cross stitch. Work the grapes coded for rose in arrowhead stitch. Work the grapes coded for blue in detached buttonhole stitch. Work the stem outline in reversible cross stitch or Montenegrin stitch. See photo on page 53.

DB 5, 6: Work Montenegrin stitch. *pg· 21 + 23*

Row 6: Work the vine in Montenegrin stitch and diagonal Montenegrin stitch. Work the tendrils in double running stitch, using dark blue. Work the leaves (green areas) of the flowers in cross stitch and double backstitch. Work the flower in rice stitch, using two colors: dark rose for the base cross stitch and light rose for the corner diagonals.

Row 7: Work the vine in Montenegrin stitch and diagonal Montenegrin stitch. Work the leaves and stems in reversible cross stitch and diagonal cross stitch. Work the inside of the leaves, point B, in chain stitch. Work the flower petal outline, point C, in Parisian stitch. Note: The colors will encroach into the area of the next color. Work the circular flower center, point D, in hollie-point stitch. Work the leaves below the flower in reversible cross stitch. Work tendrils coded for medium rose in reversible cross stitch. See photo on page 67.

DB 7, 8: Work alternating double backstitch.

Row 8: Work the vine in four-sided stitch. Work the leaves attached to the vine with a single Algerian eye stitch. Work the four sections of the flower, using satin stitch in the kloster-block style, with an eyelet center.

Row 9: Work the vine in reversible cross stitch and diagonal cross stitch. Work the center of the vine, point E, in chain stitch, using light green. Work the two sections of the blue flowers next to the vine in Montenegrin stitch to outline both sections. Work the outside leaves, point F, in satin stitch. Work the inside section of the flower in double herringbone stitch, using dark blue and light blue. Work the tendrils attached to this section in double running stitch, using dark green. Work the small leaves attached to the vine in reversible cross stitch and diagonal cross stitch. Outline the center motif in reversible cross stitch, using Smyrna cross stitch to fill the small squares, point G. Work the inside of the petals, point H, in satin stitch. Outline the lovers'-knot center in reversible cross stitch. Work the small squares, point I, within the lovers' knot in rice stitch. Work the inside of the lovers' knot, point J, in braid stitch, using gold metallic thread. Work the stem and outline of the carnation base in diagonal cross stitch and reversible cross stitch. Work the inside of the base of the carnation, point K, in trellis stitch. Outline the carnation petals in Montenegrin stitch. Work the center of the outside petals, point L, in brick stitch. Note: The colors will encroach into the next color. Work the center portion of the carnation, point M, in lattice stitch, using dark rose for the base stitch and light rose for the couching stitch. Work one vertical stitch to couch each intersection. Work the tendril in the center of the carnation, point N, in double running stitch, using dark green. Work the stem and outline of the design between the carnation and the center blue flower in diagonal cross stitch and reversible cross stitch. Work the inside of this design, point O, in Roman stitch. Work the tendrils attached to the stem in double running stitch, using medium green. See photo on page 81.

DB 9, 10: Work Williamsburg stitch using dark rose for the base color and light rose for the top color.

Row 10: Work reversible cross stitch. Work your name in this area.

DB 11, 12: Work satin-stitch sawtooth pattern, using ecru pearl cotton (coton perlé). See Illustration 5.

Row 11: Work the V-shaped row of squares in faggot stitch. Work flowers in satin stitch. Work stems in cross stitch and tendrils in double running stitch. Work the thin, rectangu-lar shapes between the rows of faggot stitch in satin stitch. Work the squares on each side of these rectangular shapes in Algerian eye stitch. Work this row using pearl cotton #12 (coton perlé), except for faggot stitch, which is worked using ecru tatting thread #80. See photo on page 93.

Row 12: Work using drawn-thread techniques. See Illustration 6. Work around the outside of the drawn-thread section in double hemstitch, using ecru pearl cotton #12 (coton perlé). Wrap the bars, dove's eyes, and weaving thread using ecru tatting thread #80. Note: Linen thread #60/2 can be substituted for the drawn-thread work in this row. See photos on pages 93 and 103.

DB 13, 14: Work satin stitch. See Illustration 7.

Row 13: Work the small squares, point P, in four-sided stitch. Work the small lines inside the four-sided-stitch sections in buttonhole-bar stitch. Work the center sections, point Q, in satin stitches with a buttonhole-stitch circle in the center. See Illustration 8. Work the small, diamond-shaped areas, point R, using a star eyelet in the center. Work this row using ecru pearl cotton #12 (coton perlé). See photo on page 103.

DB 15, 16: Work double backstitch.

Row 14: Work family initials in reversible cross stitch. Work the acorn pattern in the center in double running stitch, using medium rose. See photo on page 3.

**Color Code**

**Kreinik**
**Soie d'Alger**

| | | |
|---|---|---|
| X | 1715 | Dark Blue |
| △ | 1714 | Medium Blue |
| L | 1712 | Light Blue |
| ■ | 2916 | Dark Rose |
| •. | 2915 | Medium Rose |
| ℓ | 2913 | Light Rose |
| + | 4246 | Medium Brown |
| ◣ | 1835 | Dark Green |
| V | 1834 | Medium Green |
| S | 1832 | Light Green |
| Y | 2233 | Yellow |
| ⊙ | DMC Ecru Pearl Cotton (coton perlé) #12 | |
| G | DMC Gold Metallic | |
| | DMC #80 Brilliant Tatting Cotton | |

Fabric: 32-count vintage linen from Wichelt Imports, Inc. (Note: Cut fabric 30" x 12".)

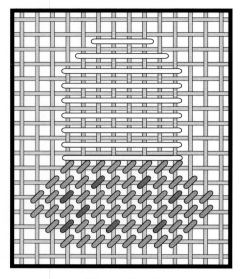

Illustration 1

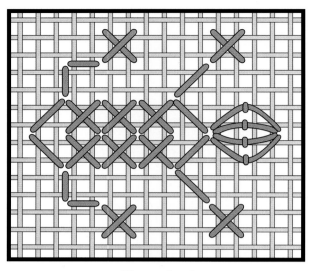

Illustration 2

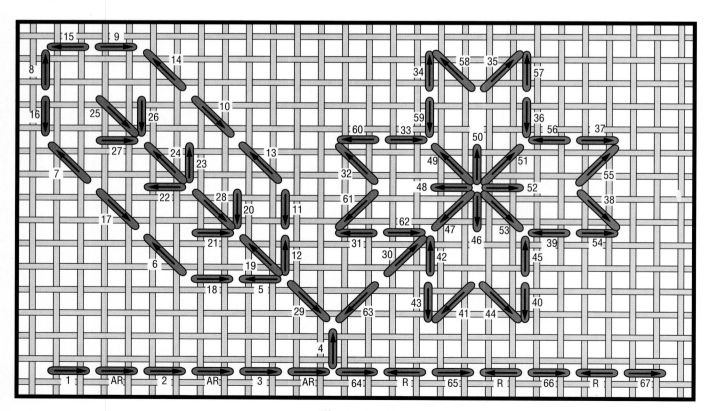

Illustration 3

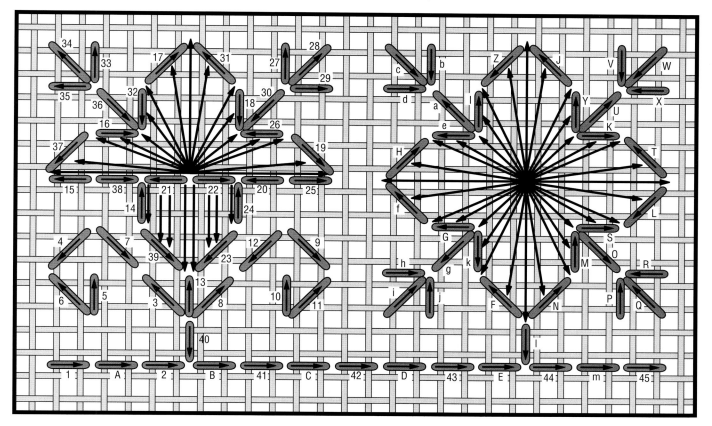

Illustration 4

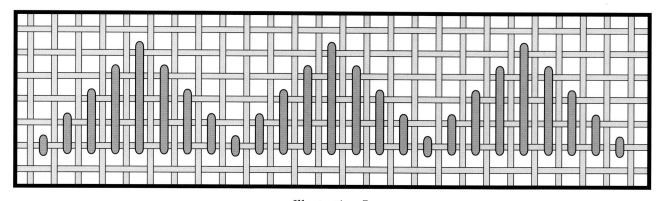

Illustration 5

Row 12

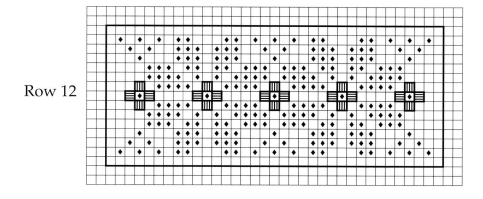

Illustration 6

125

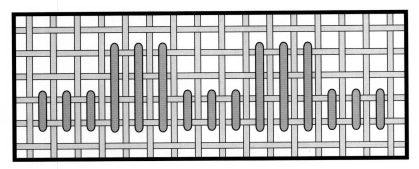

Illustration 7

Illustration 8

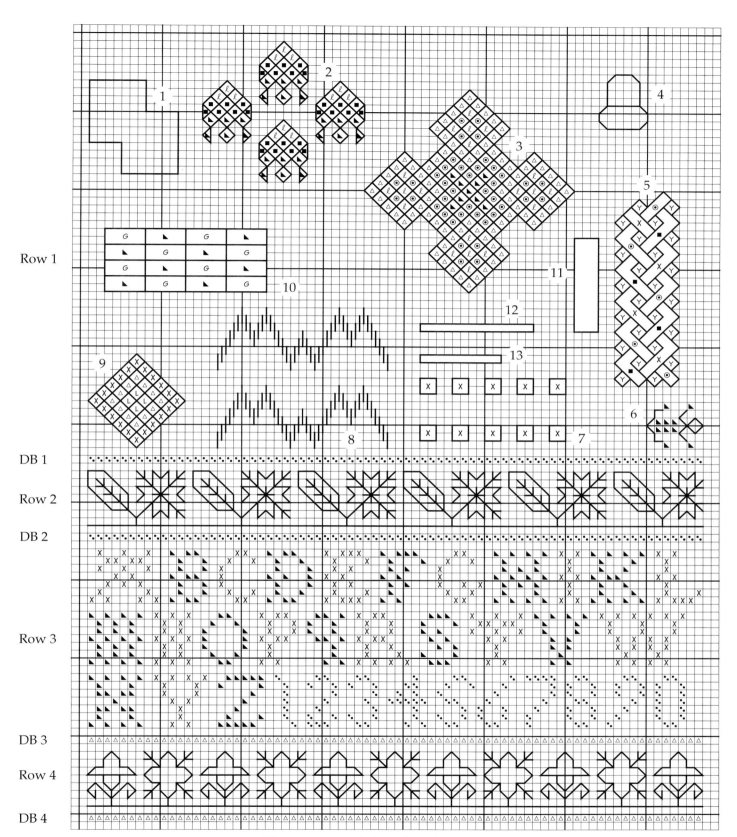

The Proper Stitch Sampler—Section 1

127

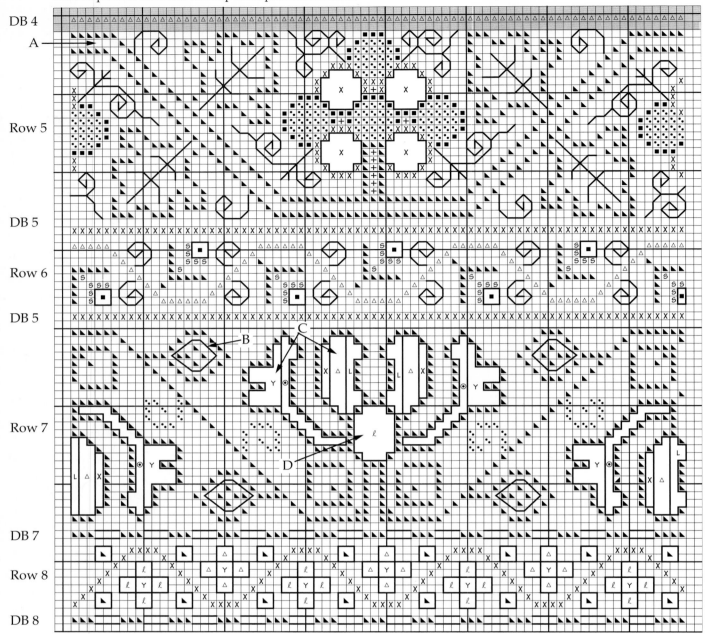

The Proper Stitch Sampler—Section 2

The Proper Stitch Sampler—Section 3

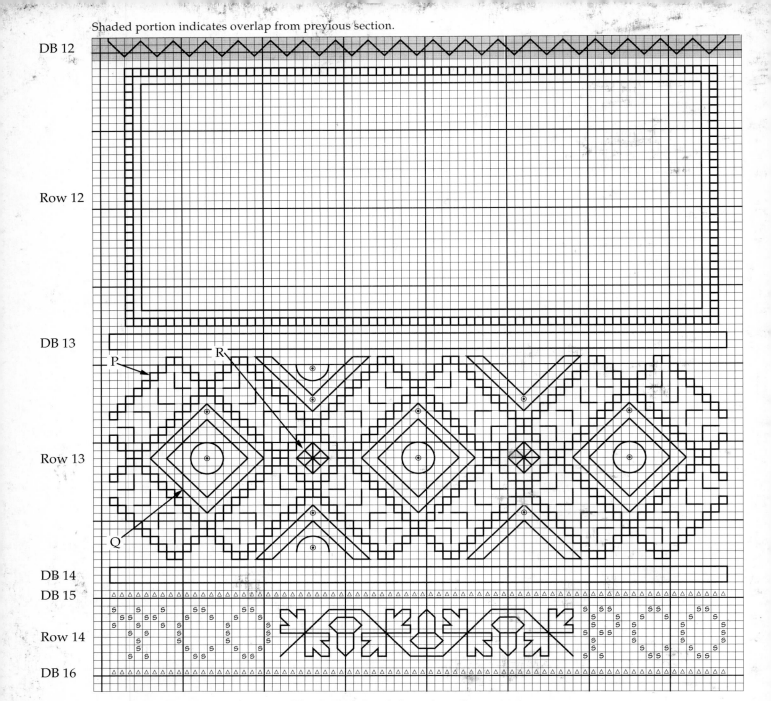

The Proper Stitch Sampler—Section 4

# Our English Heritage Sampler

Designed after the fashion of band samplers from the sixteenth and seventeenth centuries, *Our English Heritage Sampler* reflects the character of early English pieces. The model pictured uses 12 counted-thread stitches. The sampler was designed in alternating bands of color and whitework that depict common geometric patterns of the time.

Work the design from the top, starting in the upper-left corner of the fabric. Work all dividing bands; then work rows. Use one strand of silk in the needle. Refer to color code if color is not designated in instructions.

DB 1: Work this dividing band in two journeys. Complete the top in double backstitch. Complete the bottom (second journey) in double backstitch, with the center design worked in double running stitch. See Illustration 1.

DB 6, 7, 12, 13: Work in a method similar to Dividing Band 1. Use Montenegrin stitch to work the top and bottom, with double running stitch in the center. See Illustrations 2 and 3.

DB 18: Work in a method similar to Dividing Band 1, using double backstitch. See Illustration 4.

DB 2, 5, 8, 11, 14, 17: Work these dividing bands in alternating double backstitch, using ecru.

DB 3, 4, 9, 10, 15, 16: Work these dividing bands in four-sided stitch, using ecru.

Note: After dividing bands are completed, work main rows of design, beginning with row 1. Refer to color code if color is not designated in instructions.

Row 1: Work cross stitch or reversible cross stitch.

Rows 2, 4, 6, 8, 10, 12: Work double running stitch and satin stitch. These rows require two journeys to complete: numbers designate journey one and letters designate journey two. Use one strand of silk and stitch twice for satin stitch. For rows 2 and 4, refer to Illustration 5. For rows 6 and 8, refer to Illustration 6. For rows 10 and 12, refer to Illustration 7.

Row 3: Work these stitches: satin, faggot, Algerian eye, and double running. See Illustration 8 for placement of faggot stitch (diagonal squares) and satin stitch. Use one strand of silk and stitch twice for satin stitch. See Illustration 9 for path of the star pattern. For satin-stitch area, use one strand of silk and stitch twice. Work double-running-stitch tendril as reached, before finishing satin stitch.

Work both satin stitch and double-running-stitch areas before working Algerian eye. Note: When working the full design, only one tendril is stitched in the center where the two sections join.

Row 5: Work these stitches: reversible cross, diagonal cross, arrowhead, queen, double backstitch, double running, and chain. First work the vine, stem, and attached leaves in reversible cross stitch and diagonal cross stitch. See Illustrations 10 and 11. Fill the leaves using queen stitch. Queen stitches, point A, are worked using light gold. Queen stitches, point B, are worked using medium blue. Work the inside of the vine, point C, in chain stitch, using dark gold. Work the base of the carnation, point D, in arrowhead stitch. Work the outline of the carnation in reversible cross stitch, using dark rose. Work the inside of the carnation in rows, using double backstitch. Work the tendrils, point E, in double running stitch, using medium blue.

Row 7: Work these stitches: Algerian eye, satin, and four-sided. See Illustration 12 for placement of Algerian eye and satin stitch. Use techniques described for Row 3. Work the small, square areas on the chart in four-sided stitch, using ecru. See Illustration 13 for the S-shaped pattern of satin stitch.

Row 9: Work these stitches: diagonal cross, double backstitch, double running, detached buttonhole (with trailing thread), satin, running, and queen. Work the horizontal vine areas in double backstitch. (Reversible cross stitch can also be used.) Work diagonal cross stitch in the center of each section where the vine dips. Work the entwining vine section, point G, in queen stitch, using medium blue for areas labeled B and light gold for areas labeled Y. See Illustration 14 for detail of point G. After the vine is stitched, work an outline in double running stitch or backstitch on the outside of both sides of the entire vine, using dark gold. Work the two tendrils, point H, on either side of the main flower stem in double running stitch, using dark gold and working off the vine outline. Work the stem, branches, and tendrils of the flower design, point I, in double running stitch, using medium green. Include the diamond pattern at the base of the pinwheel flower and up to the acorn cap. Work the acorn caps, area J, in detached buttonhole (with trailing thread), using dark green.

Work the acorns in horizontal satin stitch, using dark rose for area K and medium rose for area L. Work an outline around the pinwheel flower in double running stitch, using dark blue. Work the diamond patterns on the four sides using medium green. See Illustration 15. Work detached buttonhole stitch (with trailing thread), area M, using dark blue. Work the center of the flower, area N, in vertical satin stitch, using light gold. Work running stitches, area O, using dark rose. Work the tendrils in each corner, area P, in double running stitch, using dark rose.

Row 11: Work these stitches: satin, faggot, and double running, using ecru. Begin in the center, working satin-stitch parallelograms to each side. See Illustration 16 for placement of faggot stitch (diagonal squares) and satin stitch acorn inside parallelogram design. Note: Acorn motif is centered in faggot-stitch area.

Row 13: Work reversible cross stitch. Work your name in this row. Add other family initials if you choose.

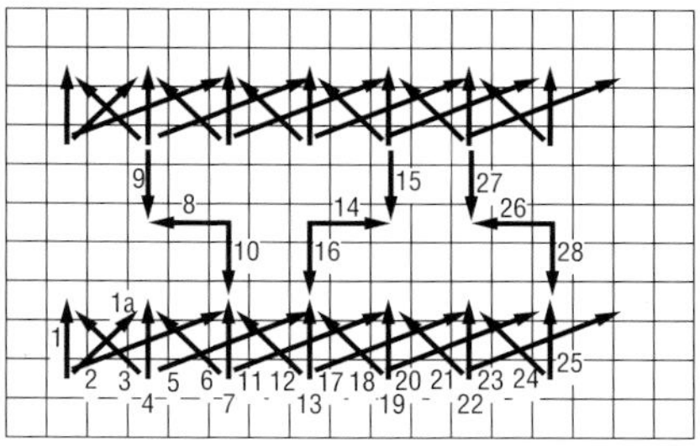

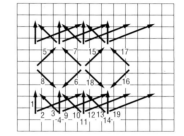

Illustration 2

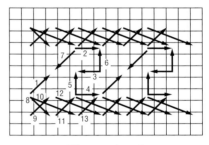

Illustration 3

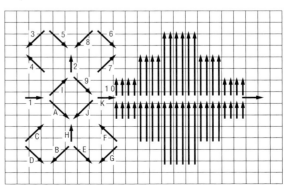

Illustration 4

**Color Code**

**Kreinik**
**Soie d'Alger**

| | | |
|---|---|---|
| ■ | 4623 | Dark Rose |
| ⊙ | 4621 | Medium Rose |
| + | 2911 | Light Rose |
| X | 1745 | Medium Blue |
| ● | 4231 | Ecru |
| ✳ | 1835 | Medium Green |
| L | 1834 | Light Green |
| O | 4234 | Dark Gold |
| f | 2131 | Light Gold |
| | 1746 | Dark Blue |
| | 1836 | Dark Green |

Fabric: 32-count raw linen from Wichelt Imports, Inc. (Note: Cut fabric 24" x 14½".)

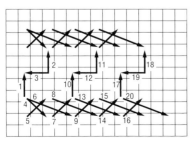

Illustration 1

Illustration 5

133

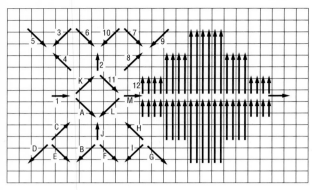

Illustration 6

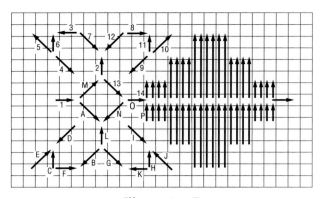

Illustration 7

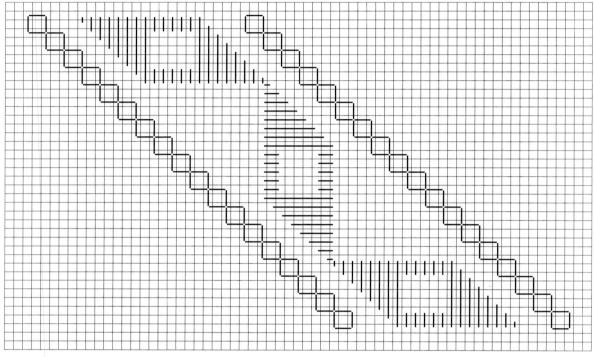

Illustration 8

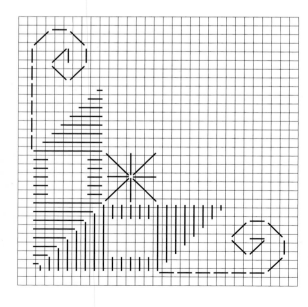

Illustration 9

Illustration 10

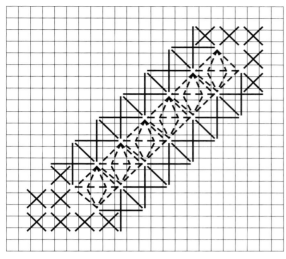

Illustration 11

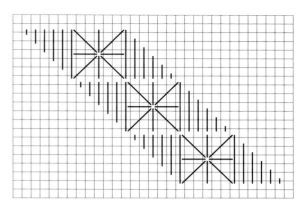

Illustration 12

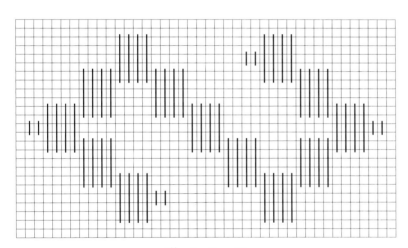

Illustration 13

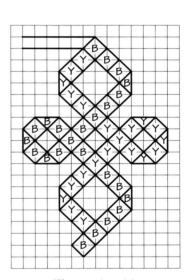

Illustration 14

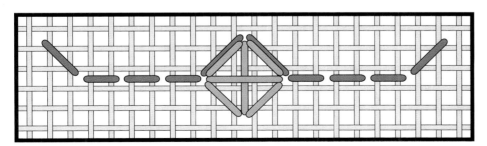

Illustration 15

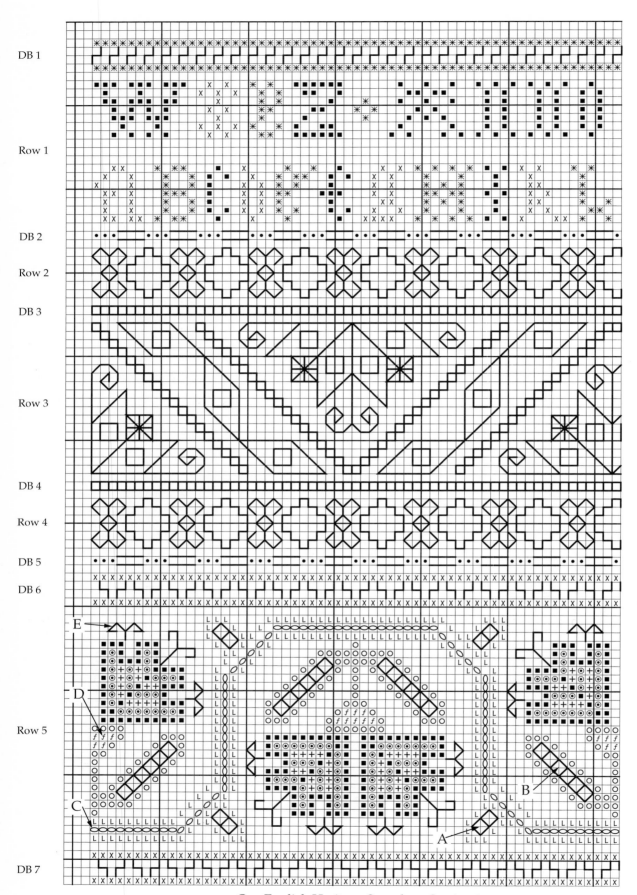

Our English Heritage Sampler—Section 1

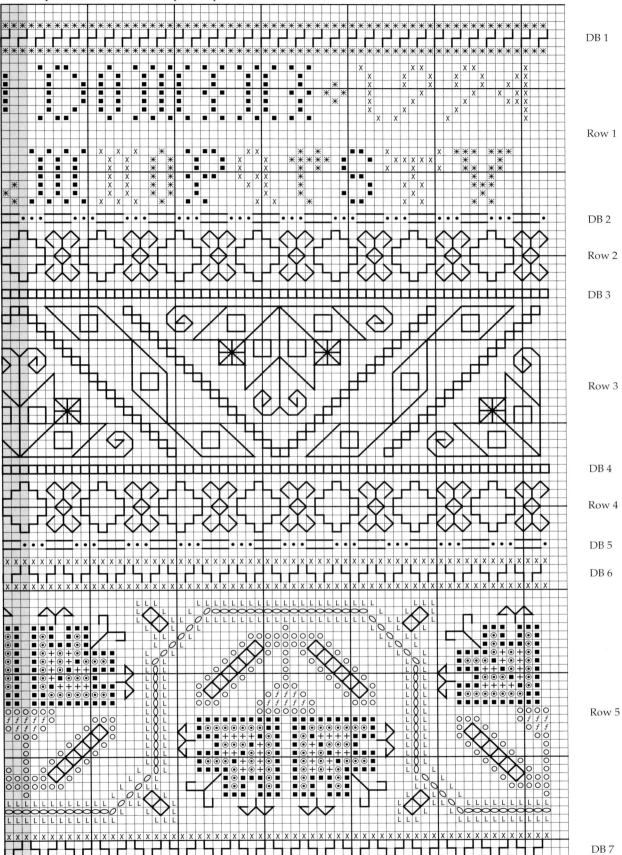

DB 1

Row 1

DB 2

Row 2

DB 3

Row 3

DB 4

Row 4

DB 5

DB 6

Row 5

DB 7

Our English Heritage Sampler—Section 2

DB 7

DB 8

Row 6

DB 9

Row 7

DB 10

Row 8

DB 11

DB 12

H

G

K

I

J

Row 9

M

M

J

N

L

M

O

M

P

DB 13

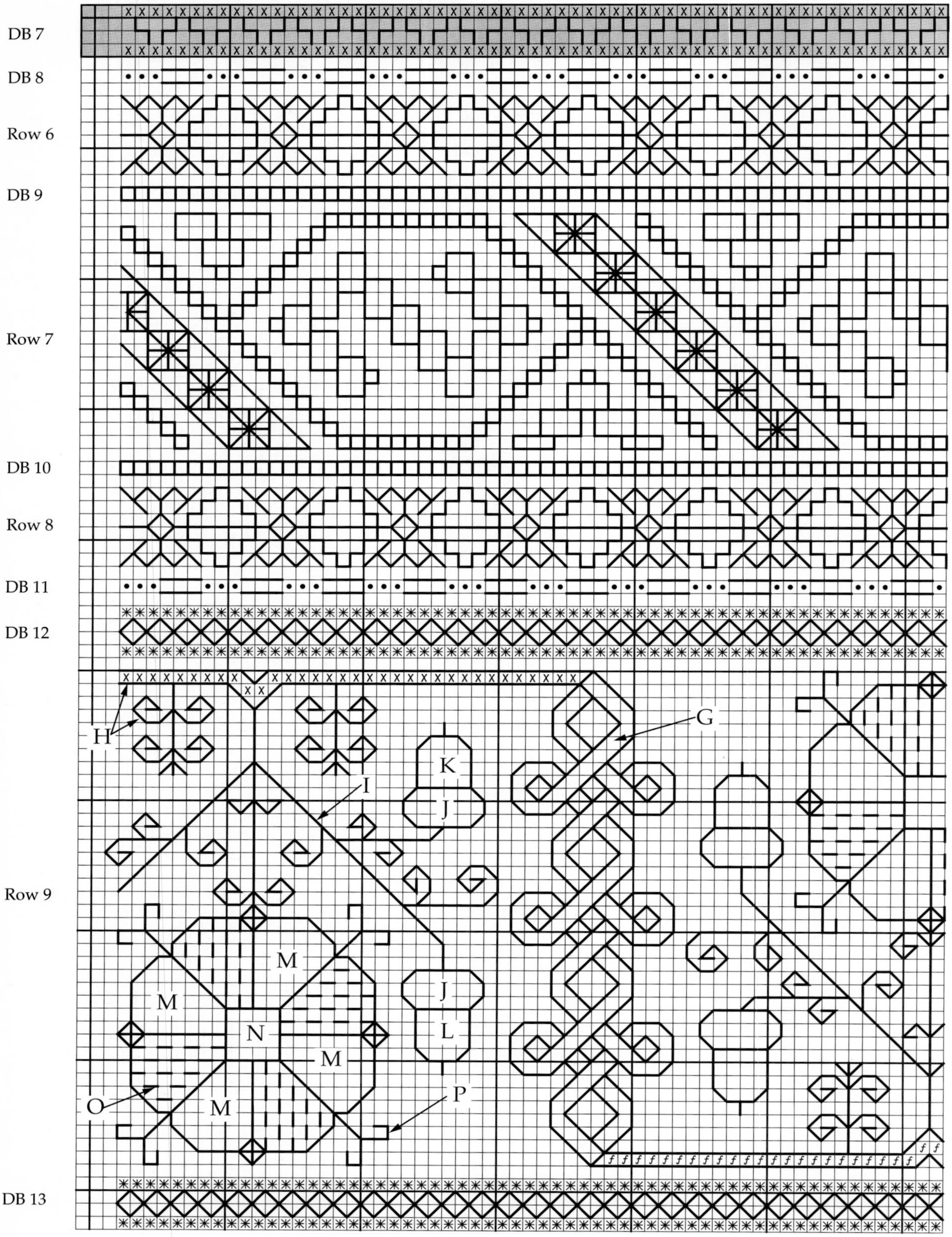

Our English Heritage Sampler—Section 3

DB 7

DB 8

Row 6

DB 9

Row 7

DB 10

Row 8

DB 11

DB 12

Row 9

DB 13

Our English Heritage Sampler—Section 4

Shaded portion indicates overlap from section 3.

Our English Heritage Sampler—Section 5

Place your name in this row.

DB 13
DB 14
Row 10
DB 15
Row 11
DB 16
Row 12
DB 17
Row 13
DB 18

Shaded portion indicates overlap from previous section and section 4.

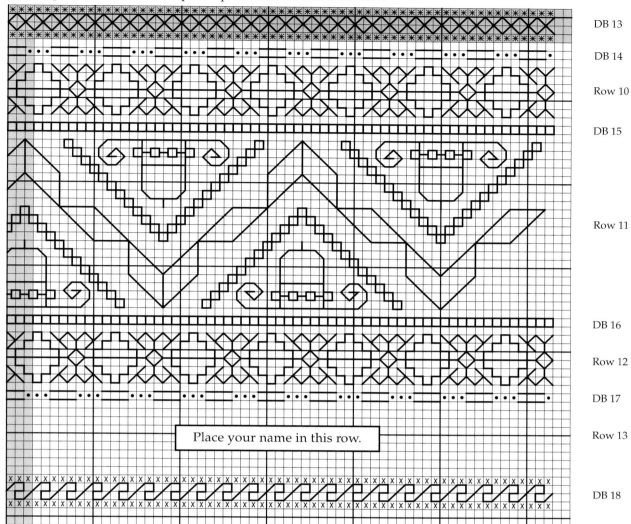

DB 13

DB 14

Row 10

DB 15

Row 11

DB 16

Row 12

DB 17

Place your name in this row.

Row 13

DB 18

Our English Heritage Sampler—Section 6

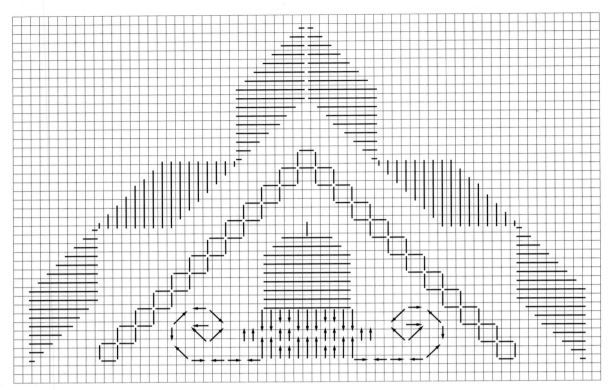

Illustration 16

| Section 1<br>DB 1–DB 7<br>Left Side | Section 2<br>DB 1–DB 7<br>Right Side |
|---|---|
| Section 3<br>DB 7–DB 13<br>Left Side | Section 4<br>DB 7–DB 13<br>Right Side |
| Section 5<br>DB 13–DB 18<br>Left Side | Section 6<br>DB 13–DB 18<br>Right Side |

Schematic

# Index

Numbers in **bold** type indicate color photo pages.

*Darlene O'Steen and Symbol of Excellence Publishers, Inc., wish to thank Frank and Sara Powell of Cross Patch, Wake Forest, North Carolina, for framing the sampler project,* Our English Heritage Sampler; *The DMC Corporation for metallic threads and tatting threads; Kreinik Manufacturing for silk floss; and Wichelt Imports, Inc. for linens.*